Science of the Soul

Dr. Bill Steinke
Mesa Az, Jan 2017

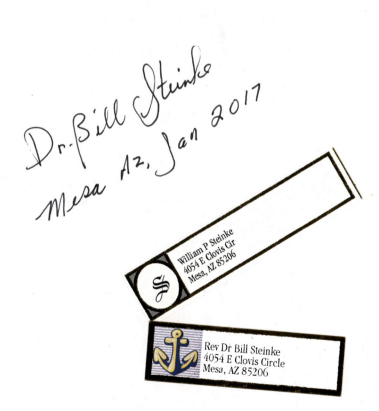

William P Steinke
4054 E Clovis Cir
Mesa, AZ 85206

Rev Dr Bill Steinke
4054 E Clovis Circle
Mesa, AZ 85206

Marie-Louise von Franz, Honorary Patron

**Studies in Jungian Psychology
by Jungian Analysts**

Daryl Sharp, General Editor

Science of the Soul
A Jungian Perspective

Science of the Soul

Encounter with the Greater Personality

The Therapeutic Life

The Vocation of Depth Psychotherapy

The Transference Phenomenon

EDWARD F. EDINGER
Edited by Daryl Sharp and J. Gary Sparks

Edward F. Edinger is the author of 14 other books in this series.
See page 126 for details.

National Library of Canada Cataloguing in Publication Data

Edinger, Edward F. (Edward Ferdinand), 1922-1998
  Science of the soul: a Jungian perspective

(Studies in Jungian psychology by Jungian analysts; 102)

Includes bibliographical references and index.

ISBN 1-894574-03-6

1. Jungian Psychology.
2. Transference (Psychology).
I. Sharp, Daryl, 1936-.
II. Sparks, J. Gary (John Gary), 1948-.
III. Title. IV.. Series.

BF175.E35 2002   150.19'54   C2002-900226-5

INNER CITY BOOKS
Box 1271, Station Q, Toronto, ON M4T 2P4, Canada

Telephone (416) 927-0355 / FAX (416) 924-1814
Web site: www.innercitybooks.net / E-mail: info@innercitybooks.net

Honorary Patron: Marie-Louise von Franz.
Publisher and General Editor: Daryl Sharp.
Senior Editor: Victoria Cowan.

INNER CITY BOOKS was founded in 1980 to promote the
understanding and practical application of the work of C.G. Jung.

Index by Vicki Cowan.

Printed and bound in Canada by University of Toronto Press Incorporated

CONTENTS

See final pages for descriptions of other Inner City Books

Editor's Foreword

The world is full of unconscious people—those who don't know why they do what they do. Edward F. Edinger did as much as anyone I know to correct this situation. To my mind, he was as true to Jung as one can be. Like Marie-Louise von Franz, he was a classic Jungian: he took Jung's message to heart and amplified it according to his own talents.

For those who find Jung himself tough going, Edinger has been the preeminent interpreter for more than thirty years. In lectures, books, tapes and videos, he masterfully presented the distilled essence of Jung's work, illuminating its relevance to both collective and individual psychology. Thus, for instance, his *Mysterium Lectures* and *Aion Lectures* are not only brilliant scholarly studies of Jung's major works, they are also a practical guide to what is going on in the laboratory of the unconscious.

Since Inner City published his book *The Creation of Consciousness* in 1984, Ed and I had more than a good publisher-author working relationship. I visited him a couple of times at his home in Los Angeles, and sent him copies of each new Inner City title as it was published. He always responded quickly with a hand-written letter giving his considered opinion.

Every year or two he offered Inner City Books a new manuscript. We took every one because they were always good meaty stuff. Clean, crisp writing, no padding, no blather. Never mind that they would never appear on the *New York Times* list of best-sellers; they fit perfectly with our professed mandate "to promote the understanding and practical application" of Jung's work. We are proud now to have fifteen Edinger books under our wing.

Personally, I loved the man. I feel privileged and fortunate indeed to be in a position to keep his work and spirit alive, to the benefit of everyone who strives to become psychologically conscious.

For this volume of essays we are indebted to Edward Edinger's long-time companion, Dianne D. Cordic, for her encouragement and cooperation. We believe that the many readers who have appreciated his other books will be delighted with this one.

Daryl Sharp

Acknowledgments

"Science of the Soul" was originally a three-part video series, taped in Los Angeles in April 1995. The audio portion has been transcribed and edited by J. Gary Sparks. Thanks to Christopher Albrecht for permission to publish this work. The videos distributed by Desert Spring Media are available from the C.G. Jung Bookstore, Los Angeles.

"Encounter with the Greater Personality" was a lecture presented to San Diego Friends of Jung in September 1984. A transcription by Joan Dexter Blackmer has been edited for this book.

"The Therapeutic Life" was originally a lecture given in 1962 to Jungian analysts in New York and Los Angeles. A version entitled "The Relation between Personal and Archetypal Factors in Psychological Development" was published in *Psychological Perspectives,* vol. 19, no. 2 (1988). It has been newly edited for this book.

"The Vocation of Depth Psychotherapy" is an edited transcription by J. Gary Sparks of a lecture given in September 1996 to analysts and trainees at the C.G. Jung Institute of Los Angeles. An earlier version was published in *Psychological Perspectives,* vol 35 (1997).

"The Transference Phenomenon" was a paper presented in October 1956 at a meeting of the Analytical Psychology Club of New York. The version published in *Spring 1957* has been edited for this volume.

1
Science of the Soul

Man has always lived in the myth, and we think we are able to be born today and to live in no myth, without history. That is a disease. absolutely abnormal, because man is not born every day. He is born once in a specific historical setting, with specific historical qualities, and therefore he is only complete when he has a relation to these things. If you grow up with no connection with the past, it is just as if you were born without eyes and ears. . . . [and] that is a mutilation of the human being.[1]

The Collective Unconscious

For an individual to be psychologically healthy, one must have a living connection to the collective unconscious. Throughout history that connection has been provided by the operative religion or mythology that functions in a given society. A particular religion or living mythology functions as a container of the collective unconscious. The person who believes in a living myth has access to dogmas, ceremonies and symbolic images that stand between us all and the raw reality of the collective unconscious. That is the function served by religion and living myth.

As long as one is related to such a religious myth, one doesn't have to pay any attention to the psyche. The religious institution takes care of it, and if you're a good member, if you're living in containment within its dogmatic structure, you're saved. There is the old saying, you know, that there's no salvation outside the church. That's true, there is no salvation outside of *a* church, *a* living mythology, except the process of individuation, and that is rare and difficult.

So as a kind of general truth, it's more or less true that there's no

---

[1] Jung, "The Houston Films," in William Maguire and R.F.C. Hull, eds., *C.G. Jung Speaking*, p. 348. [The Edinger videos have brief clips of Jung talking, here printed in italics, taken from interviews later published in *C.G. Jung Speaking.*—Ed]

salvation outside the church, and it doesn't matter what church we're talking about. You see, as long as you have a container for the collective unconscious, and the individual is an earnest member of some religious congregation, then one is saved, psychologically. One has a relation to the God-image in projection. As Jung has said, the great religions are great psychotherapeutic systems. That's what they are, and they provide for their members a connection to the God-image, the Self (Self and God-image being virtually synonymous terms), via the rituals and dogmas of the given church

As long as that method works, there is nothing to be said against it, but there is no such thing as depth psychology as long as one is contained in a church. As long as the collective unconscious is bound, so to speak, to the symbolism of a concrete, particular religious dogmatic structure, there's no possibility of experiencing it empirically and individually. There is no depth psychology for those who are contained within a specific religious creed because there's no need for it. Depth psychology has been born in the modern age because many do need it. We have to have it.

Many nineteenth-century poets—Nietzsche, Matthew Arnold and others[2]—announced the fact that the prevailing traditional Christian mythology no longer served its function, and modern individuals were no longer contained. At the least, the creative minority of Western society has fallen out of containment in the Christian myth, and therefore it is open and available to the possibility of empirically discovering depth psychology.

The Age of Transformation

A major change took place in collective psychology about the fifteenth century. The way I like to put it, in somewhat dramatic form, is that "God fell out of heaven into the psyche."[3] It was about that

---

[2] [See Jung, *Nietzsche's* Zarathustra: *Notes of the Seminar given in 1934-1939,* and Edinger, *The Mysterium Lectures: A Journey Through Jung's* Mysterium Coniunctionis, pp. 222ff.—Ed.]

[3] [See Edinger, *The Aion Lectures: Exploring the Self in C.G. Jung's* Aion, esp. chaps. 9, 10, 23.—Ed.]

time that the collective projection of the deity into the metaphysical realm of religious dogma was withdrawn. It was a slow process, and it started in only a few people at a time, but it really started then. The God-image fell out of metaphysical projection and into the psyche. What we saw then was a collective inflation, a vast increase of ego energy that manifested itself everywhere. People started exploring the globe, and making all sorts of discoveries in science and art. There was a great expansion of human consciousness on the ego level. But that was paid for by a progressive loss of connection to the transpersonal dimension, a process now reaching its culmination.

The human ego has so taken charge of psychic energies that the reality of the objective psyche, the reality of the transpersonal dimension of the psyche, which used to be vouched for by religious and metaphysical convictions, is now largely inoperative as an effective factor in collective life. That condition has reached such an extreme that, as I see the unfolding picture, it's the harbinger of the next eon. This state of affairs was predicted in the Christian Bible, in the Book of Revelation, where it is all laid out symbolically.⁴

The discovery of depth psychology in the twentieth century is in my opinion at least as significant as, and equal in magnitude to, the discovery of nuclear physics. Look what has happened. For thousands of years, humanity has had the concept of the soul, of the psyche, of an elementary awareness that human subjectivity is a very significant factor, but humanity has been so close to that reality that they couldn't treat it in an empirical or scientific way.

The image I like to use is that of fish swimming in a pond. There's a lovely anecdote, an Eastern anecdote, I came across once. The Zen master asks the novice, "Who discovered water?" The novice doesn't know, so the master replies, "Well, I don't know either, but I know who didn't discover it: the fish."

You see, human beings are in exactly that same situation in relation to the psyche. They live in it. It's their medium of being, and there

---

⁴ [See Edinger, *Archetype of the Apocalypse: A Jungian Study of the Book of Revelation.*—Ed.]

are little glimmers of light where individual egos exist in that general medium of the psyche, but they are so close to it that they cannot recognize it as an empirical object that can be studied the same way nature can be studied—as an object. But what happened with the discovery of the unconscious, with Freud and Jung, was that suddenly the psyche became an object to the perceiving subject ego. And that then opened it up for scientific study. This is really a huge Copernican revolution that has as yet hardly penetrated collective awareness.

Jung and Freud

We really owe the empirical discovery of the unconscious to Freud. He studied cases of hysteria, and out of that study discovered the unconscious. Jung, at just about the same time, although he was nineteen years younger than Freud, was conducting experiments that discovered the unconscious from another angle. He was doing experiments on the word association test which revealed what Jung called unconscious complexes.[5] So when Jung started reading Freud, he realized that they were both dealing with the same phenomenon, and they arranged to meet. Their meeting was an historic encounter.

> *Oh, well, I just paid a visit to him in Vienna and then we talked for thir-*
> *teen hours without interruption. . . . We didn't realize that we were al-*
> *most dead at the end of it. . . . I was then a very young man still, and he*
> *was the old man and had great experience and he was of course way*
> *ahead of me and so I settled down to learn something first.[6]*

For some years they were colleagues. Though one was in Vienna and the other in Zürich, they met frequently and had a lot of discussions. There were always differences, but for a long time Jung subordinated his own thinking to Freud's, because he was aware that Freud had more experience than he did. But that all changed following the publication in 1912 of Jung's *Transformations and Symbols of the*

---

[5] [See *Experimental Researches*, CW 2 (CW refers throughout to *The Collected Works of C.G. Jung*).—Ed.]

[6] Jung, "The Stephen Black Interviews," in Maguire and Hull, eds., *C.G. Jung Speaking*, p. 253.

Libido.[7] There was a parting of the ways then, because Jung was coming into his own and he was aware that there were serious differences in the way each of them understood the psyche, especially in terms of libido, or psychic energy.

> *That book cost me my friendship with Freud, because he couldn't accept it. To him the unconscious was a product of consciousness, and simply contained all the remnants; it was a sort of store-room where all the things consciousness had discarded were heaped up and left. To me the unconscious then was already a matrix, a basis of consciousness of a creative nature, capable of autonomous acts.*[8]

Jung then went through a profound experience of the unconscious, from 1914 to 1918, and it was at that time that he made the personal, immediate discovery of the collective unconscious. Freud had discovered the unconscious, but just its personal dimension, which is certainly real enough. But the contents of Freud's unconscious had reference only to the individual's personal life, one's childhood in particular, whereas the collective unconscious, Jung discovered, opened up the vista of the individual psyche immensely. This is so because it reveals that the individual psyche is floating, so to speak, on an ocean that is shared by our whole species.

The Nature of Dreams

What are dreams and how are we to understand them? Here again, there is a profound difference between the views of Freud and Jung. They agreed that the dream is the royal road to the unconscious, but they disagreed as to the destination of that road. Freud thought it led to the discovery of wish-fulfillments, and that the symbolic nature of dreams was to be accounted for by postulating a censor of some kind. Jung didn't buy that at all; he considered the dream to be a product of nature. Nature doesn't deceive, she just speaks her own language, and

---

[7] [The literal rendering of the original 1912 German edition, *Wandlungen und Symbole der Libido*, would be *Transformations and Symbols of the Libido*, though in English it was called *On the Psychology of the Unconscious*. In a significantly revised 1952 edition, the book became *Symbols of Transformation*, CW 5.—Ed.]

[8] Jung, "The Houston Films," in Maguire and Hull, eds., *C.G. Jung Speaking*, p. 339.

it's up to us to learn that language, to come to an understanding of it.

Dreams do speak a symbolic language that one has to acquire the ability to understand. There are different levels of dreams, too—surface dreams and depth dreams, little dreams and big dreams. Big dreams have archetypal images in their content. The smaller dreams seem to derive from the personal unconscious, and the bigger dreams have more than a personal relevance. They are relevant to an entire community, or society, because the archetypal factors that determine individual existence are also operative in the broader collective. And it is indeed true that there can at times be absolutely astonishing wisdom revealed in dreams, wisdom not only of the present and the past, but sometimes wisdom of the future.

Jung has demonstrated that the unconscious operates beyond the categories of time and space. This means that a relevant event referred to by a dream could take place in the future rather than the past, that the future event is casting its shadow backward, so to speak. Those things are hard for the rational ego to accept, but the data is very clear that they do happen.

The Creation of Consciousness

Consciousness is one [factor], and there is another, equally important, the unconscious, that can interfere with consciousness any time it pleases. Of course I said to myself, "Now this is very uncomfortable, because I think I am the only master in my house." But I must admit that there is another somebody in that house that can play tricks.[9]

When we seek a definition, we are trying to conceptualize an experience or an entity. The very word itself, "concept," carries the image of grasping it. And in order to grasp something, you have to have a sizable enough reach to incorporate it. But many of these basic entities are so large that they are ungraspable by rational means, and all we can do then is talk around them, circumambulate them, look at their different aspects.

So let me try to do that with the entity we call consciousness.

---

[9] Ibid., p. 340.

All we know about consciousness is what individuals experience; it's a term describing an experience. And if you reflect on the experience, then you can start to say something about it. It is often helpful to reflect on the initial versions of a given experience, so we might consider the initial versions of consciousness. For instance, in his autobiography Jung describes his boyhood experience of coming to consciousness at about the age of eleven. One day, suddenly, it was as though he walked out of a mist and realized, "I am myself now, now I exist."[10] Previously, that awareness had just never come to him.

Consciousness means, for one thing, awareness. And it means not only awareness of objects, because even animals have that; animals don't run into objects, they are aware of them and steer clear of them, and when they see you they recognize you and keep their distance. So they are aware of objects, but they are not aware of themselves. That's the crucial feature of consciousness: consciousness is aware of itself, it is the ego being aware of itself. When Jung walked out of his mist and realized "I am," at that moment the ego was perceiving itself as an object.

That's the great mystery of consciousness, that it has the reflective power to look in the mirror and see itself as a separate image. It is not just fortuitous that Yahweh in the Old Testament states his identity as "I am."[11] I think there's a connection between the psychology of consciousness and the symbolic image of Yahweh. See what happens with the revolutionary discovery that "I am." It's a birth, you see, the birth of a light that didn't exist before, and what it brings with it is an enlarged awareness of the sovereignty of the ego.

In the course of realizing that it exists, the ego simultaneously realizes that it exists in surroundings, and that there are objects and other people that likewise exist. At the same time one realizes that inner consciousness is a separate realm that can't be penetrated; it is

---

[10] *Memories, Dreams, Reflections*, pp. 33f. [See also "The 'Face to Face' Interview," in Maguire and Hull, eds., *C.G. Jung Speaking*, p. 425.—Ed.]

[11] Exod. 3:14. [See Edinger, *The Bible and the Psyche: Individuation Motifs in the Old Testament*, p. 48.—Ed.]

inviolate. This is the source of the symbolism of the king, the recognition that consciousness brings with it a sense of sovereignty. And this is the sense that has expanded so tremendously in Western society for the last five hundred years: the ego's sense of its sovereignty in relation to nature and the world.

Consciousness in the Unconscious

We're talking about consciousness and its various aspects. This brings up another question, namely "Is there consciousness in the unconscious?" And the answer is, "Yes, there is." Jung discusses this matter in his very important essay "On the Nature of the Psyche,"[12] where he points out that the consciousness in the unconscious is diffuse and partial. It does not have the focused clarity that ego consciousness has; it is of a different nature, probably best described as latent consciousness. That also means that the unconscious is a subject.

Part of the phenomena of consciousness is the discrimination between subject and object. I am aware of being a conscious being; I am the subject of that awareness. When I look out into the world I see objects, and in the process of separating myself from identification with those objects, there is a separation of subject and object. That is the way consciousness develops, by splitting subject from object. I am the subject, and what I have to deal with outside is the object of my perception.

Now the same thing happens in the inner world. One discovers that the unconscious has contents that are objects to my subject. And I can perceive them as objects, and speak of them as the objective psyche. But then can we also say that the objective psyche that I perceive as an object is a subject in itself, that perceives me as an object? And the answer is, "Yes, we can." Just by definition, if consciousness exists it has to have a subject, it has to have a seat to reside in. That's the meaning of the word subject.

To the extent that we grant that the unconscious psyche has consciousness, we grant that it is a subject in itself, which can look out at

---

[12] *The Structure and Dynamics of the Psyche,* CW 8.

me and relate to me as an object. It is that phenomenon that is expressed symbolically in the notion of the Eye of God.[13]

You see, one of the features of the experience of the Self is being looked at by the Eye of God. A very disquieting experience, to be examined with utter objectivity by an inner subject that's treating you as an object. When one is being treated as an object, one is no longer the sovereign. As long as you're the subject, you're the sovereign, the sovereign one who's surveying his realm. But when you're the object, then the subject that is looking at you is the sovereign surveying *his* realm, and that gets us into all the symbolism that is associated with the archetype of the Last Judgment.

The Structure of the Psyche

Persona

Every model of the psyche has to start with the ego. The ego is the seat of consciousness and the subjective center of one's sense of identity, so everything that exists in consciousness must be related to an ego, to a subject. That's the starting point.

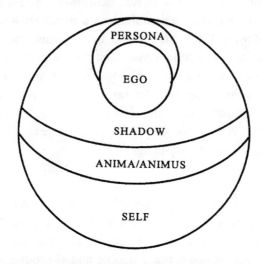

---

[13] [See Edinger, *The Creation of Consciousness: Jung's Myth for Modern Man*, esp. pp. 42ff.; also Edinger, *The Mysterium Lectures*, pp. 218f.—Ed.]

Then, according to Jung's model, looking outward from the ego to the outer world, there is a function, an entity, that he calls the persona. That's the Latin word for an actor's mask, and it is part of the word personality. That psychological function allows the individual to function as a hypocrite. I use that word specifically because *hypocrite* is the Greek word for actor, and that's what we all are when we operate through the persona. Of course it's also a function of adaptation, a mark of relatedness to our environment, to accommodate ourselves to what others expect. But the result is that every profession tends to develop its own persona. So you have a medical persona, an ecclesiastical persona and so on. Of course analysts have personas too, the analytic persona, being a blank projection screen, though it is not one that Jungian analysts approve of.

So the persona is the psychic entity that operates between the ego and the outer world. Now when you look in the other direction, inside, what one encounters first is the shadow. That is the inferior side of the personality in which resides what the individual considers to be the undesirable, dark and even evil aspects of oneself. Usually we do not acknowledge them because it is too demoralizing. That is the first thing one encounters when one undergoes a depth analysis. Below that one finds what we call the anima and the animus, the anima representing the feminine image in a man, and the animus representing the masculine image in a woman. The projection of animus or anima often accounts for the experience of falling in love or, conversely, extreme dislike. Behind those images are the Great Mother and the Heavenly Father. And at the very core of the psyche, if one gets that far, is the Self, the inner God-image.

Shadow

Let us start with a consideration of how the shadow is created, because that is the background for its integration. During childhood and youth, as the ego develops, it is vitally important that it establish a sense of autonomy vis-à-vis other people and the outer world. That's why at a certain stages of childhood, there is so much no-saying.

You see, we have to be able to say No in order to establish our separateness from others. The ego cannot be formed by perpetual agreement. It doesn't get established that way. So, as the ego develops, it says, "No, I don't like this, I do like that"; it says, "No, I am not this, I am that; I am good, I am not bad." And as it makes all those discriminations, it creates the shadow, the container for what it is not.

It is vitally important for a young ego to feel that it is more good than it is bad. If it falls into the conviction that it is more bad than good, it's a goner. Then it starts living out of that, and you get criminality and all sorts of antisocial behavior. So the ego has to be convinced that it's more good than bad. But then what happens to all of those so-called bad qualities that it denies having? They drop into the shadow, into the unconscious.

Over and beyond the personal shadow, there is also the archetype of the shadow. In Judeo-Christian culture, it is often personified by the devil. When the personal shadow is unconscious, it merges with the archetypal shadow; then there is no clear discrimination between the personal and the archetypal, and one is open to the possibility of actually succumbing to possession by the archetype of evil.

But somewhere about the middle of life, if one is meant to develop, that process of relation to shadow has to be reversed. One needs to begin to reclaim all those negative and inferior qualities that one rejected in the earlier course of ego formation. But that *is* a dangerous business. It's dangerous because if one is inundated too abruptly with shadow qualities, and comes to the realization, "I am really not the good person I thought I was, I really do have all these very despicable qualities," it can be very demoralizing.

How does one safeguard oneself from falling into the archetypal shadow? I only know of one sure way, and that is to be aware of the existence of the archetypal shadow as distinguished from the personal shadow. In other words, just an intellectual understanding of these different components of the psyche can be very protective. Because then, hopefully the idea will come to mind: "Oh yes, I read about this in Jung, I understand what it is and I've been warned that I shouldn't identify with it."

Anima and Animus

The archetype is a force. It has an autonomy and it can suddenly seize you. It is like a seizure. Falling in love at first sight is something like that. You see, you have a certain image in yourself, without knowing it, of woman, of the woman. Then you see that girl, or àt least a good imitation of your type, and instantly you get a seizure and you are gone. And afterwards you may discover that it was a hell of a mistake. A man is quite capable, he is intelligent enough, to see that the woman of his "choice," as one says, was no choice, he has been caught! He sees that she is no good at all, that she is a hell of a business, and he tells me so. He says, "For God's sake, doctor, help me to get rid of that woman!" He can't, though, he is like clay in her fingers. That is the archetype, the archetype of the anima. . . . It's the same with the girls. When a man sings very high, a girl thinks he must have a very wonderful spiritual character because he can sing the high C, and she is badly disappointed when she marries that particular number. Well, that's the archetype of the animus.[14]

Jung says that the assimilation of the shadow is the minor task or opus and assimilation of the anima is the major one.[15] It is not too hard to come into some awareness of one's shadow; that is within the range of possibility of most people, given some instruction and assistance. It seems to be much harder, however, to make the anima or animus conscious.

Not a few people who ought to know better don't even acknowledge the empirical existence of the anima and animus. They think they are just concepts, ideas that one could just as well do without. But they are not just concepts, they are living psychic organisms which one will recognize and be aware of only if one has had the experience that makes you aware. But it does require quite a bit of insight to come to that awareness.

---

[14] Jung, "The Houston Films," in Maguire and Hull, eds., *C.G. Jung Speaking*, p. 294.

[15] ["If the encounter with the shadow is the 'apprentice-piece' in the individual's development, then that with the anima is the 'master-piece.' " (*The Archetypes and the Collective Unconscious*, CW 9i, par. 61).—Ed.]

I'll speak first of the anima in a man.

The anima is a rich, complex and ambiguous entity that has many different aspects. She reaches deep down into the collective unconscious and has a profoundly archetypal aspect. The anima also embodies all of the man's significant experience of women. That is all built into the anima image, so that it becomes a fateful entity. Fate is one of the key words that is applicable to a man's anima. When the anima is activated, one can know that something fateful is going to happen to him for good or for ill.

As with all archetypes, the anima is a paradoxical union of opposites. She is simultaneously a whore and the Virgin Mary. She has powers, profound powers, of seduction and allure, spiritual guidance and elevation. She can both tempt a man to his total destruction and lead him to his highest fulfillment. That is the range of her capacities, and needless to say a rational ego alone cannot encompass an entity of such magnitude. But that's what she is.

Let me repeat: this is not a concept, it is a living empirical reality that can be demonstrated if you care to look through the telescope of depth psychology. (I'm thinking of Galileo's telescope that people refused to look through because they didn't want to know that Jupiter had moons.) The anima's initial major manifestation is almost always in projection. A man meets a woman who catches his eye, and he falls in love. That phenomenon is an anima projection. Try to tell that to him at the time and you won't get very far. But it can be demonstrated. That is not to belittle the experience, not by any means; calling it a projection means that its power derives from inside rather than from outside, but in no way does that diminish its importance.

Sometimes the projection can happen all at once, as in love at first sight, but it can fall off all at once, too. One only needs to see the fallibility or personal defects of the actual woman shine through, just once, and that may be enough for the whole projection to collapse, gone in a puff. In which case, it means that the fateful element of the projection has not been activated. When the fateful element of the anima is activated, when it's found to reside in a particular woman, then that woman becomes that man's fate, for good or for ill, and twist and turn as he might, she's got him. A classic example of that is *Carmen,* the opera, but the examples are of course all over.

Now the other way the anima can manifest herself is by possession of the ego, rather than by alluring the ego through outer projection. If the ego falls into a state of identification with the anima, then the man becomes a kind of effeminate, resentful whiner. That is not uncommon. When the anima manifests as ego-possession, her negative qualities prevail; there is no solid, functioning ego to relate to her. What happens then is that the ego falls into regressive, infantile behavior of one sort or another; the mother aspect of the anima is activated internally, and the ego expects mothering from all concerned. In less extreme versions we have what are called anima moods, which often surface at times of conflict in relationships. The woman falls into an animus mood, which I'll mention in a moment, and the man is prey to an anima mood. The animus mood is characterized by aggressive opinionating, and the anima mood by resentful complaining.

Now let's speak about the animus.

Much of what I said about the anima applies equally to the animus in a woman. You see, both these images are rooted in the Self, and therefore they really have the God-image at their core, or one face of the God-image. Put them together, put them in a syzygy, a yoked-together pair, and then you have the combination, the *coniunctio,* the two faces of the God-image.

Like the anima, the animus is made up of a combination of archetypal and personal factors. And often, just as the personal mother has a contribution to make to the man's anima, so the father sizably contributes to the actual image of the woman's animus. The same fateful factors apply, the same ambiguity, the same union of opposites.

The animus is on the one hand the highest kind of spiritual guide, or savior, and on the other hand he's a violent rapist. The two sides are both contained in one image. It is no small task for a woman to integrate those two images, to recognize them as a unity. It is a major psychological achievement to reach that degree of integration, to be able to see beyond the opposites, to recognize that they are two sides of the same phenomenon. But they are.

As a general rule, the animus has more to do with mind and the anima has more to do with heart, so knowledge of these figures and how they function in the psyche are extremely helpful in understanding what happens in intimate relationships.

You see, in every relationship between the sexes there are actually four players: the man's ego and the woman's ego, the man's anima and the woman's animus. This can be illustrated as follows[16]:

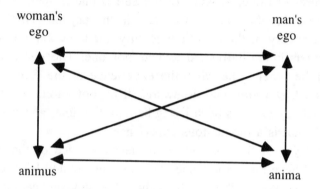

When a man and woman like each other and start up a relationship, there will first of all be a relationship between them on a conscious level. The man consciously likes what the woman is, and vice versa, and they start relating on that level; that's the first and obvious level. But then the other players enter the picture; if there's going to be anything of depth between them, the man's anima is projected, attached to the woman, and the woman's animus is projected onto the man. Then you have a more complex interchange, because the man is seeing not only the woman he is conscious of, but also his anima projection; and the woman sees not only the man she is conscious of, but also her animus projection.

It then becomes more complicated still, because the animus of the woman sees the man's anima and starts having a reaction to that, and the man's anima sees the woman's animus and reacts to that. So you

---

[16] [Diagram adapted from Jung's drawing in "The Psychology of the Transference," *The Practice of Psychotherapy,* CW 16, par. 422.—Ed.]

see it can really be quite a complex interchange. When two people get into disputes or misunderstandings, an awareness of this structural phenomenology is a help in sorting out the problems.

The Self

The Self is a very big subject indeed. It is what you come to if you penetrate all the way to the core of the collective unconscious. One of the features of the experience of the Self is that it opens one up to the awareness that there are two centers in the psyche. That's a momentous discovery of the twentieth century, made by Jung, that there are two centers in the individual psyche, not one. The ego is one and the Self is the other. And when the experience of the Self erupts in the individual, suddenly one is aware: "I'm not alone in my own house, somebody else has been living here all the time, and I've never known it." That is a momentous experience.

The prototype of this, of course, is the experience of the external other; we all have that experience very early in life and learn to adjust to it. The very young child realizes that it is not the center of the universe, that there are other centers that claim equal consideration. That then leads to the whole phenomenon of the socialization of the ego, the realization of an outer other. The experience of the Self is the inner version of that experience, and sometimes the impact is so great that it shatters the ego. It can generate psychoses, this kind of experience. But when the ego is sufficiently developed to be able to take the experience, then it is possible to assimilate it.

Now, what often happens is that if there is some religious or mythological system at the disposal of the individual, the experience will be assimilated into that particular religious formulation, and it will be described as an experience of God, within the precepts of that religion. But what we now have, for the first time, is the opportunity to create an empirical science concerning this level of psychic reality. Always before we've had innumerable creeds of one kind or another, but we've never had an empirical science of this phenomenon, and this is what Jung has made available to us.

Individuation

Individuation is a term used extensively by Jung to describe the whole psychological process in which the ego becomes progressively conscious of its own nature, its background and the ground on which it's rooted. Another way of putting it is that individuation is the process whereby the ego comes into a conscious awareness of, and relation to, the Self; or that it is the process whereby the individual ego undergoes a differentiation from its collective identities.

The concept of individuation covers a very sizable area. The word has the same root as individual, which means it is easy to confuse individualism with individuation. I'm very fond of Emerson, and he's relevant to this whole question because he was the great American exponent of the dignity and amplitude of the individual. He is often misunderstood because people think he preaches a kind of egotistical individualism. But he doesn't. It is clear from his essays that he had the intuitive awareness of what Jung calls the Self. You find that in his essay "The Over-Soul,"[17] for instance.

The nineteenth century did not yet have the conceptual awareness of the two different centers of the psyche, and therefore egocentric behavior and Self-centric behavior could not be distinguished. That leads to confusion and the misunderstanding of thinkers like Emerson. But individuation is not individualism. Individualism is the aggrandizement of the ego, whereas individuation refers to the process whereby one discovers the reality of the Self, the second center of the psyche, and then relates one's way of life to that connection.

The classic paradigm in the Christian myth for this kind of experience is the conversion of Paul on the way to Damascus.[18] He experienced an encounter with the Self, symbolized by the image of Christ, and it transformed his life. From then on, he was no longer an ego-centered man, he was Self-centered. He called the Self Christ, because that was the imagery by which he assimilated the experience. And thereafter in his letters he would describe himself as "slave of Christ."

---

[17] *Emerson's Essays*, essay ix.
[18] Acts 9.

(The English translation softens that and calls it "servant," but in the original it is *d'u'ls,* which means slave.) That's the effect of a decisive encounter with the Self. It generates a contact with an authority that carries an divine kind of quality, so that one feels compelled to serve it. The result is that it relativizes the ego. That's the major consequence of individuation, and very different from individualism.

I spoke earlier of the ego being like a fish in a pond, and unaware of the medium it lives in. In the same way, the primitive and immature ego exists mainly in identification with its surroundings. It has only a feeble awareness of its individual existence. The majority of the energies and effects of the psyche are experienced as external. This is expressed in what we speak of as the animistic phase of religion, when animating spirits are perceived as existing in one's surroundings. Certain trees or animals have an animating spirit in them, and a primitive person having to make an important decision may say, "I must go out and consult my tree spirit," or "I must go and consult my snake who lives in a hole beside my hut." These are all examples of what we call animism, and they illustrate the fact that the primitive psyche is exteriorized—the individual is spread out all over the place.

Something similar happens in modern people in the early stages of ego development. We all start out identified with our environment and with the people in it. That's what makes the opinions of others so extraordinarily important to young people—their psyche resides in those others.

Now the process of individuation, as Jung conceives it, is a process whereby one progressively collects those pieces of oneself and "returns" them to the container where they belong. Well, "return" isn't quite the right word because they were never there in the first place, but anyway "transfers" them from their external locations into the containing unity of the individual psyche. And as one does that one discovers remarkable things. One discovers that one is different from the group, from one's friends, from one's spouse.

You know, as long as we identify with other people, or with another person, we just assume, automatically without any reflection, that certain basic qualities and experiences are shared. So it comes as quite a revelation to discover that no, the other person is quite separate, with very different experiences and perceptions, a whole different world, in fact.

These discoveries are all part of the process of individuation in which one progressively discriminates oneself from the initial *participation mystique*—that's a technical term used in Jungian psychology, borrowed from the sociologist Lévi-Bruhl,[19] because it so aptly describes the state of the primitive ego in identity with its surroundings. Relatively mature people should not flatter themselves that they are free of *participation mystique,* because, believe me, we're not. All our lives, we constantly discover little pockets of *participation mystique,* where we have made assumptions of identity, when in fact we are dealing with profound individual differences.

Alongside the process of differentiating one's individual identity and reality from others and from the environment, at the same time one also differentiates oneself from inner factors. That disidentification proceeds, you see, as the analytic process reveals the inner factors as objects.

Once an inner factor is perceived to be an object for scrutiny, then it is perceived in its separateness and the ego can no longer identify with it. Then one can be aware of the shadow, and relate to it, without falling into identification with it, or without projecting it. Projection and identification are two versions of the same phenomenon. Likewise, when one becomes aware of the animus or anima, one no longer falls either into an identification with the image or into a projection. The same thing is true with the Self.

So, these are the procedures, and they are long-term procedures. Individuation is a life task, and it can only be accomplished when a significant amount of energy is applied to it. It is not a part-time job because it is the life process itself; it incorporates everything that takes place in our lives.

---

[19] [Claude Lévi-Bruhl (1837-1939) was a French philosopher whose study of the psychology of primitive peoples gave anthropology a new approach to understanding irrational factors in social thought, primitive religion and mythology.—Ed.]

Social Implications

As one progresses in the process of self-knowledge, what does it mean to learn about each of those items, those functions, that go to make up the structure of the psyche as I've described it?

The ego is the starting point for everything. One of the goals of the life process, the natural life process as well as the analytic process, is ego development. One can have no real analysis, no real confrontation with the unconscious, until one has a sturdy, responsible and ethical ego. Before that there is no question of depth analysis, only supportive psychotherapy to promote ego development.

It is vitally important, in terms of a stable social structure, that members of society have good, strong, reliable egos. That means they have to have an authentic sense of their own identity; they have to have acquired a character structure that enables them to function responsibly in relation to other people. That is all a product of ego development. So, to start with, ego development is good not only for the individual but also for the society. *Family & Friends*

Awareness of the Persona

Now, of what value is awareness of the persona to the individual and society? Here again, as with all self-knowledge, both the individual and society benefit. You see, it commonly happens that, to a greater or lesser extent, one is identified with one's persona. It is so convenient. It is hard enough to acquire competence in a professional career, and once that has been achieved, the satisfactions of that achievement are often so significant that there is a strong tendency to identify with that professional role.

So the minister learns an appropriate persona as he goes through theological seminary, and then starts his first job as assistant pastor; the medical student learns the medical persona, the lawyer learns hers, and so on. And once that is learned, things work so smoothly when operating out of it that there's a strong tendency to identify with it. But the trouble is, for society as a whole, that when one meets one's doctor, or one's pastor, or one's lawyer, or whatever, one isn't meeting a full human being. You meet the mask.

I can tell you that it's a real problem in the medical profession. Doctors are very busy and it takes too much time to be real. It is much easier to function out of your medical persona. The great advantage of it, though temporary, is that it doesn't take any effort, you don't have to respond out of the deeper human realities. So you can get a lot more work done in a day; you can see more patients. It takes much more time to listen to them and respond humanly, and then you get way behind in your schedule.

All that is understandable. But if self-knowledge is to proceed and if individuals are going to achieve a full, well-rounded personality, it is important that they realize the reality of the persona and the fact that it is not identical with the ego. If they happen to identify with it now and then, they must understand that they are diminishing themselves. Once those things become clear, then the initial identification is broken, and even though you may choose to operate out of the persona at times, you know what you are doing. It makes a world of difference whether you're doing something consciously or unconsciously, because choice is involved.

Awareness of the Shadow

Turning to the next item, the shadow, what is the social advantage of being aware of the shadow? I can tell you that it is immense, because as long as one is unconscious of the shadow, it is projected, usually onto a person or group that provides some hook, some quality that, maybe only to a small degree, corresponds to the nature of one's own shadow. When that happens, the projector has the delightful experience of locating evil. It's out there, in *you*. Now I know what to attack in order to make the world a better place. In lesser shadow projections perhaps no great harm is done. It's simply an abrasion in the general mechanics of ordinary human relationships. But once it starts operating on a collective scale, shadow projection is disastrous.

I hardly need to give examples of this, because they can be seen wherever you have one faction opposing another and attributing dark, evil, if not diabolical, intentions to the enemy. We see this everywhere. It is the consequence of shadow projection, and it is really a disgrace in this day and age for a supposedly mature human being to be caught engaging in crude shadow projections. But disgrace or not, it happens all the time and does grave damage to our social fabric.

So, to the extent that an individual, through the analytic process or otherwise, becomes aware of his or her shadow, one is less likely to project the shadow. One recognizes that the particular quality, or idea or mode of living that is so annoying in the other person is actually an expression of one's own shadow, which accounts for the annoyance. We can have likes or dislikes, but when a certain level of affect enters the picture, that's an infallible indication of a shadow projection. Those who are unconscious of their shadow are a grave danger to the welfare of society as a whole.

Awareness of Animus and Anima

Here we come to a deeper layer of the unconscious, where the social aspects cannot be spelled out in such simple terms. They are present, but they are much more complex. Certainly we can say that someone who has even a rudimentary awareness of the reality of the anima or animus will relate to the opposite sex in a more authentic, more conscious, more fruitful and realistic manner.

After all, the relationship between the sexes is quite fundamental to the whole social process. The family is based on it, and the raising of children, their welfare and early psychological development, is largely dependent on the level of conscious relationship that exists between the parents. The type of understanding relationship that can endure the inevitable conflict between the opposites benefits by an awareness of the animus and anima. With that awareness, one avoids the crudest of projections and can relate to the partner in terms of his or her reality rather than in terms of the illusory expectations one has when one projects the anima or animus onto the partner.

Awareness of the Self

As described earlier, the Self is the center and totality of the psyche. One of its synonyms is the inner God-image. It is the transpersonal authority of the psyche. The ego is the smaller authority, the Self the larger authority. When one has made contact with the Self, the ego then becomes relativized; it recognizes that its life must be governed by an authority higher than itself.

Now, what does such a recognition have to do with society? A great deal indeed. In a certain sense we can say that society is the exteriorized mirror of the individual psyche. Every society has a leader of some sort—a king, a president or prime minister. Occasionally it's an oligarchy of aristocrats. But always, in order for a society to be cohesive and organic, it must have a central authority, and that central, external, social authority is a mirror of the inner authority of the Self. That is why when one dreams of a king or a president or of a capital city, in most cases those dreams refer to the Self.

What is at issue here is the individual's relation to authority. If one has no connection to the Self, and particularly when the ego is weak, when there is a low level of psychological differentiation—especially in times of social turmoil and distress—there is a strong tendency for the Self, the central organizing authority principle of the psyche, to be projected.

In times of turmoil the compensatory aspect of the psyche is activated; disorder constellates order, and in such circumstances order is often imposed with a level of discipline and authoritarianism.

What can happen in such cases is massive collective projections of the Self onto the leader, a *Führer* for instance. That happened in Nazi Germany, which is an instructive lesson of a magnitude that can hardly be exaggerated in terms of the danger of the projection, the collective projection, of the Self. We also see it happening in all sorts of charismatic religious cults, and on a smaller scale everywhere. As we lose our containment in our conventional religious myth, this danger grows. It is the greatest threat to humanity, far greater than the nuclear bomb.

Transformation of the God-Image

Jung puts this concept very succinctly in "Answer to Job" when he says, "Whoever knows God has an affect on Him."[20] Now that's a symbolic statement. In psychological terms, the Self needs the ego, and the ego's awareness and relation to it, in order to be transformed. That puts it in our neutral psychological language.

The Self or God-image in its unconscious form, as I've said before, is a paradoxical union of opposites. This is the ground of our psychological being, and the Christian God of love is only one half of it. That is why Satan has never disappeared; he leads a separate existence, but he is still around. Jung has demonstrated that Christ and Satan are the two sons, the two opposite sons, of the same paradoxical deity.[21] And when these images come into the range of empirical experience they require some reconciliation. They generate an inner conflict that is intolerable until it achieves a reconciliation, and this is what happens when the individual encounters the primordial God-image in its paradoxical oppositeness. It experiences the activation of the conflict within the nature of the godhead. But also contained within the whole dynamic is the potential for a union of those opposites, which can often be achieved in the individuation process through active imagination. The net result then is that the psyche is no longer split.

The Christian psyche is split, and that means everybody. Whether you're a professing Christian or not is irrelevant; it is part of the collective psychology we all share, so we're all split because the God-image is split. In fact, the split occurred even before Christianity; it was split by Plato and the Stoics, so that it has a philosophical source too. But that split, that paradoxical doubleness of deity, is what undergoes reconciliation and transformation when an individual human consciousness engages this depth issue in his or her own individual life. Then that little piece of the collective psyche that is carried by the

---

[20] *Psychology and Religion,* CW 11, par. 617. [See also Edinger, *Transformation of the God-Image: An Elucidation of Jung's* Answer to Job, pp. 60f.—Ed.]
[21] [See ibid., pp. 11, 81, 121f., and Edinger, *The Aion Lectures,* pp. 56f.—Ed.]

individual has been transformed. If enough individuals have this experience and thus participate in this transformation of the God-image, then they act as a kind of leaven to society as a whole, and very gradually, a new collective God-image is born out of that.

You know, this question often comes up in modern thinking, "Is Christianity doomed? Has it run out?" Jung makes a very interesting point in that regard. He points out that the Christian myth itself contains, as part of its thematic structure, the death of God. I want to see if I can spell this out, because I think it is of some importance.

According to the Christian myth, and I elaborate on this in my book *The Christian Archetype*,[22] God descends to earth by incarnating himself as a man, through the agency of the Holy Spirit who impregnates the Virgin Mary. God as man then lives a human life on the earth. He goes through the passion, he dies, he is resurrected and then ascends to heaven. So that in his incarnated form the myth describes the deity as passing through a death. What then happens after his death, according to the Christian myth, is that the Holy Spirit descends again on Pentecost. And this time, according to the dogma, the Church is born. Pentecost is considered to be the birthday of the Church. So the incarnation cycle repeats itself: the Holy Ghost, the deity, descends and is incarnated a second time in the Church, which describes itself as the body of Christ.

Then, according to certain theologians,[23] the Church as the body of Christ is obliged to live out the same fateful sequence as did Christ. That means the Church must also go through a passion and a death. Now the Church projects those events onto the last days, as far off as possible. But psychologically we might consider that it is happening right now. With the Church as the body of Christ, the collective incarnation of Christ so to speak—Christ was the first individual incarnation, the Church was the second, collective incarnation, which must also go through the passion and the death, and resurrection—now, according to my understanding, the resurrection will then initiate a

---

[22] [See esp. pp. 128ff.—Ed.]
[23] [For example, the Catholic theologian Hugo Rahner. See ibid., pp. 17, 128.—Ed.]

third cycle, in which the Holy Spirit will incarnate itself in individual human beings.

That's Jung's point. And as you see, when I spell it out that way, it is a consistent and quite appropriate continuation and reinterpretation of the Christian myth. Jung was in fact very concerned that the treasure of the Christian myth not be lost to modern man. What he provided is a transformative reinterpretation of it in his notion of continuing incarnation, which preserves all of the rich Christian symbolism, but now understood on an individual, psychological level. That is my understanding of what the new epoch means, and why Jung is, in my view, an epochal man.

We are in for some very grave disturbances in the collective social fabric of Western society. Jung was keenly aware of that, and he even made the remarkable statement, in a letter, that he wrote "Answer to Job" because he did not want to allow things to drift toward the impending catastrophe.[24] What he revealed there, and expressed very clearly, is that "Answer to Job" is the antidote to the apocalypse. If one can understand "Answer to Job," one would be in a position psychologically to survive the onslaught of the apocalypse, of the transition from one epoch to another.

What this means, without summarizing the whole book, is that a process is going on in which the God-image is undergoing transformation, and the process of that transformation requires human awareness of the divine nature in order for that nature to change. That puts it in a nutshell. I'll repeat it. The essence of "Answer to Job," which could allow one psychologically to survive the apocalypse, is the realization that the apocalypse is a process in the transformation of God in which, by means of entering human consciousness, the divine nature can change. This is all spelled out in the Bible in the Book of Job. I also discuss it in my book on Blake's series of engravings for the Book of Job.[25]

---

[24] *Letters*, vol. 2, p. 239.
[25] [See *Encounter with the Self: A Jungian Commentary on William Blake's* Illustrations of the Book of Job, esp. pp. 53ff.—Ed.]

ck.

You see, part of the divine nature (and remember I'm speaking psychologically, not metaphysically) is that the God-image is a union of opposites. It is not only Christ, it is also Satan. It is not only Yahweh of the Book of Job, it is also Behemoth and Leviathan. And that paradoxical God-image, with its dual nature, is in the process of transformation through being experienced by human consciousness. Being seen by human consciousness is the agent of its transformation, one individual at a time. It is not done collectively, not in committee; it's done in one lonely individual at a time, in those who experience the divine ambiguity, and in the process of that experience penetrate that paradoxical Self with human consciousness. That is what transforms it. This is the process I see now in its initial phases, and which I believe will continue with more and more intensity in the collective.

Experiences of the nature of the Nazi holocaust are psychological events, expressions of the collective human psyche. They are not natural disasters, they don't fall out of heaven; they are psychological events, phenomena illustrating the nature of the collective psyche. That is what is in store for as we go through this catastrophic transformation of the divine image from one age to the next.

The world hangs by a thin thread, and that thread is the psyche of man. Nowadays we are not threatened by element catastrophes. There is no such thing in nature as an H-Bomb—that is all man's doing. We are the great danger; the psyche is the great danger. What if something goes wrong with the psyche?[26]

---

[26] Jung, "The Houston Films," in Maguire and Hull, eds., *C.G. Jung Speaking*, pp. 303f.

The Annunciation to the Virgin, by Mathis Nithart
(Isenheimer Altar, 16th century; Kolmar, Unterlindenmuseum)

2
Encounter with the Greater Personality

Some years ago I talked to you about the Book of Job, with a special emphasis on Blake's engravings for that book.[27] What I have to say tonight is a logical continuation of that subject, namely the theme of the ego's encounter with the Self, regulating center of the psyche

This is the basic feature of Jungian psychology—the ego and how it relates to the reality of the Self. Jungian psychology is the only psychological standpoint that operates out of an awareness that there are two centers in the psyche. Some other psychologies, some other analytic approaches, have an awareness that there are two entities in the psyche; there is an unconscious and there is a second entity. But no other psychological standpoint operates out of the awareness that there are two *centers*. That is unique to Jungian psychology. And since there are two centers, if that comes to conscious realization, then those two centers must collide, they must have an encounter with each other. That happens when the ego, which is the little center, has an encounter with the Self, the big center.

All psychological analysis is no more than a prelude to this experience, the encounter with the Self. Here is how Jung put it:

> Analysis should release an experience that grips us or falls upon us as from above, an experience that has substance and body such as those things which occurred to the ancients. If I were going to symbolize it, I would choose the Annunciation.[28]

Now, it may very well happen that this crucial experience, although it is prepared for by analysis, does not take place during the period of regular analysis at all. It may take place many years later. In such a case one is very grateful for having some conscious knowledge

---

[27] [Published as *Encounter with the Self: A Jungian Commentary on William Blake's* Illustrations of the Book of Job.—Ed.]
[28] *Seminar 1925*, p. 111.

of Jungian psychology. One has a road map, so to speak, that helps one find one's bearings when this experience falls from above. One can then say with Job, "I have heard of thee by the hearing of the ear: but now mine eye seeth thee." [Job 42:5, King James] That's what happens when one has such an experience.

It can also occur without benefit of any analysis at all, and it can happen without any particular preoccupation with the unconscious. That is why I consider it vitally important to talk about the Self in public. You can never know when you are speaking to a person who has had or is going to have that experience, and such a person may recall what has been spoken about and may find it extremely helpful in a time of need. I know for a fact that such things do happen.

So we're going to be talking about the Self, but just what is it?

The Nature of the Self

As I said, the Self is the second center of the psyche, the ego being the first. To say a little more about it, one could say that it is the objective center as opposed to the subjective center. It is the transpersonal center, which includes both consciousness and the unconscious.

This is not a theory, it's a fact. One has to use words to describe the facts, but I assure you that what we're talking about is a fact that is verified by the experience of many people. But the Self is exceedingly difficult to describe. This is because it is a transcendent entity that is larger than the ego, which means it cannot be grasped, cannot be totally embraced, by the ego. Therefore it cannot be defined. What can be defined has to be smaller than the ego doing the defining. It is contradictory and paradoxical so far as the ego's categories of understanding are concerned. And like the Philosophers' Stone of the alchemists, it has many different synonyms which express different facets of this complex reality. One of the synonyms Jung proposed for the Self is the Greater Personality, and that is the particular entity I shall discuss tonight.

Jung introduces the term in his essay "Concerning Rebirth," where he speaks of individuation "as a long-drawn-out process of inner transformation and rebirth into another being," and goes on:

May need to mature in haste before dying

This "other being" is the other person in ourselves—that larger and greater personality maturing within us . . . the inner friend of the soul. That is why we take comfort whenever we find the friend and companion depicted in a ritual, an example being the friendship between Mithras and the sun-god. . . . It is the representation of a friendship between two men which is simply the outer reflection of an inner fact: it reveals our relationship to that inner friend of the soul into whom Nature herself would like to change us—that other person who we also are and yet can never attain to completely. We are that pair of Dioscuri, one of whom is mortal and the other immortal, and who, though always together, can never be made completely one. The transformation processes strive to approximate them to one another, but our consciousness is aware of resistances, because the other person seems strange and uncanny, and because we cannot get accustomed to the idea that we are not masters in our own house. We should prefer to be always "I" and nothing else. But we are confronted with that inner friend or foe, and whether he is our friend or our foe depends on ourselves.[29]

That's where Jung first introduces the term Greater Personality, but in that same essay he describes the ego's encounter with the Greater Personality in these very important words:

When a summit of life is reached, when the bud unfolds and from the lesser the greater emerges, then, as Nietzsche says, "One becomes Two," and the greater figure, which one always was but which remained invisible, appears to the lesser personality with the force of a revelation. He who is truly and hopelessly little will always drag the revelation of the greater down to the level of his littleness, and will never understand that the day of judgment for his littleness has dawned. But the man who is inwardly great will know that the long expected friend of his soul, the immortal one, has now really come, "to lead captivity captive" [Eph. 4:8, King James]; that is, to seize hold of him by whom this immortal had always been confined and held prisoner, and to make his life flow into that greater life—a moment of deadliest peril![30]

This final phrase comes as a shock. After hearing the beautiful de-

---

[29] *The Archetypes and the Collective Unconscious,* CW 9i, par. 235.
[30] Ibid., par. 217.

scription of the ego's encounter with the Greater Personality, we learn only at the very end that the encounter is dangerous, deadly dangerous. This refers to the wounding effect that the Self has on the ego at the first encounter. At the worst, the meeting of ego and Self can set off an overt psychosis. Even at best, the ego's first decisive meeting with the Self brings about a painful humiliation and demoralizing sense of defeat. As Jung puts it in another place, *"The experience of the self is always a defeat for the ego."*[31]

This experience of wounding or defeat is part of what I have spoken of as the Job archetype.[32] I've used that term because the story of Job is a particularly apt example of the pattern—and the chief features of this pattern are four:

1) There is an encounter between the ego and the Greater Personality represented as God, angel or superior being of some kind.

2) There is a wound, or a suffering of the ego, as a result of this encounter.

3) In spite of the pain, the ego perseveres and endures the ordeal, scrutinizing the experience in search of its meaning.

4) As a consequence of that perseverance, there is a divine revelation, by which the ego is rewarded with an insight into the transpersonal psyche.

To repeat: There is an encounter, a wounding, a perseverance and a revelation.

I'm going to give you four examples of this theme. They vary, each example emphasizing one particular aspect, but taken all together they provide a broad picture of the nature of the phenomenon. Each individual who has this experience has it uniquely; it will not be exactly like Job's or the Apostle Paul's, and it will not be exactly like Nietzsche's or anyone else's. But having various examples will help you to recognize it when you encounter it for yourself.

A lengthy list could be culled from human cultural history, but just

---

[31] *Mysterium Coniunctionis,* CW 14, par. 778 (italics in original).
[32] [See Edinger, *Transformation of the God-Image: An Elucidation of Jung's* Answer to Job, pp. 29ff.—Ed.]

to give you a brief glimpse here are a few: Jacob and the angel of Yahweh, which I shall talk about; Arjuna's encounter with Krishna, which I shall talk about; Paul's encounter with Christ; Moses' encounter with El Kidhr, the Green One, which you can find in the 18th Sura of the Koran; Faust's encounter with Mephistopheles in Goethe's *Faust;* Captain Ahab and the encounter with the whale in Melville's *Moby-Dick;* Nietzsche's encounter with Zarathustra, which I shall talk about; and finally, the one closest of all to us, Jung's encounter with Philemon as described in his autobiographical book, *Memories, Dreams, Reflections.*

I shall confine myself here to the four involving Jacob, Arjuna, Paul and Nietzsche. In making this kind of overview you must forgive the summary way in which I treat each example. It's really quite unfair to treat so briefly such profound episodes in the cultural history of the human race. My justification for doing so is to give you a sense of the archetype, and I don't know any better way to do that than to present brief individual examples. They will at least give you a sense of the underlying general symbolic image that operates within individual variations.

Jacob and the Angel of Yahweh

This account is found in the 32nd chapter of Genesis. You will recall that Jacob tricked his brother Esau out of his birthright and then, conspiring with his mother Rebecca, he stole his father's blessing, which rightfully belonged to Esau, the elder son. Jacob then had to flee the country to escape his brother's vengeance. Many years later, having two wives and considerable wealth, the time had come for him to return to his own country. But that return meant he must now meet Esau, the brother he had wronged many years previously, and naturally he was afraid.

We are always afraid of the person we have wronged. And on the night prior to the meeting with Esau he met the angel of Yahweh at the ford of the river Jabbok. The Jerusalem Bible gives the following account of this event:

And there was one that wrestled with him until daybreak who, seeing that he could not master him, struck him in the socket of his hip, and Jacob's hip was dislocated as he wrestled with him. He said, "Let me go, for day is breaking." But Jacob answered, "I will not let you go unless you bless me." He then asked, "What is your name?" "Jacob," he replied. He said, "Your name shall no longer be Jacob, but Israel, because you have been strong against God, you shall prevail against men. . . ." And he blessed him there.

Jacob named the place Peniel, "because I have seen God face to face," he said, "and have survived." The sun rose as he left Peniel, limping because of his hip. [Gen. 32:24ff.; Jerusalem Bible]

This story contains all four of the features I spoke of. There is an encounter with a superior being, a wounding, a perseverance and finally there is a divine revelation. The revelation in this case is first of all the blessing, and secondly the investment with a new name, a second identity. Jacob's collective identity is revealed because he now becomes the ancestor of Israel.

What is particularly interesting psychologically about this example is that it illustrates that an encounter with the Greater Personality may come at the same time as an encounter with the shadow. Jacob also experienced the later meeting with Esau very much as an encounter with God. Esau became for Jacob a kind of stand-in for God. That is because Jacob's guilty conscience imbues Esau with divine power. The scripture specifically says that when Jacob meets Esau he says to him, "I have seen thy face, as though I had seen the face of God" [Gen. 33:10; King James], so that Esau and God overlap. Psychologically, this means that the shadow, when unrelated to, may activate the Self, and if one has wronged the shadow, then what is activated is the Self in its avenging aspect. This motif can operate internally or externally.

In an outer, external sense, if I commit a wrong against another person, I will fear that person's desire for revenge. I know that he is entitled to revenge because I wronged him, and that condition then constellates the Self. " 'To me belongeth vengeance,' saith the Lord." [Deut. 32:35; King James] The whole phenomenon of vengeance belongs to the transpersonal center of the psyche, to the Self, and if an individual has been wronged in any serious way, it activates a defensive response from the Self. If someone has set the Self against you, you're at a sizable disadvantage.

In a similar way, if I have violated the inner figure that constitutes my shadow, this can arouse the vengeance of the Self against the ego, and all sorts of things may then happen—I may cut myself on my electric saw, or have an accident with the car; anything of that sort can happen if that constellation has been set up.

Now, what Jacob is obliged to do in this situation is encounter the reaction that has been constellated, and endure it without succumbing either to defensive hostility or to despair. If he succeeds, that would correspond to a successful wrestling with the angel. One way of thinking of it is that perhaps Jacob had to wrestle with his rage at Esau before he could arrive at a conciliatory attitude. We know that he did come to a conciliatory attitude because he sent Esau gifts, and it worked, but he could not do that until he had overcome his power reaction. The power reaction could express itself either in rage against Esau for causing him trouble, or in cringing fear of Esau because he knew Esau had a legitimate complaint against him.

Jung makes a very profound observation about this, found in his *Symbols of Transformation:*

> [The god] appears at first in hostile form, as an assailant with whom the hero has to wrestle. This is in keeping with the violence of all unconscious dynamism. In this manner the god manifests himself and in this form he must be overcome. The struggle has its parallel in Jacob's wrestling with the angel at the ford Jabbok. *The onslaught of instinct then becomes an experience of divinity,* provided that man does not succumb to it and follow it blindly, but defends his humanity against the animal nature of the divine power. It is "a fearful thing to fall into the hands of the living God." [Heb. 10:31; King James][33]

What he's saying here is that intense affects are manifestations of the Greater Personality. One should never take personal responsibility

---

[33] CW 5, par. 524 (italics added).

for an intense affect. One doesn't crank up something like that. It falls out of heaven, or roars up from the depths. Any intense affect is a manifestation of the Self—"the onslaught of instinct"—and if one can relate to it with that understanding then it becomes an experience of divinity, as was achieved by Jacob's wrestling with the angel.

Another aspect of such an encounter is mentioned by Jung:

> A contemporary Jacob . . . . would find himself willy-nilly in possession of a secret that could not be discussed, and would become a deviant from the collectivity.[34]

This corresponds to the fact that an encounter with the Greater Personality is necessarily a secret; one can't talk about it, at least not in its particulars. It's a secret that both creates the individual as something separate from the collective, and at the same time is a wound that painfully separates and alienates one from the collective, so it has both a positive and a negative aspect.

A striking example of this phenomenon is the figure of Philoctetes in Greek myth. Philoctetes inherited the golden arrows of Heracles, who in the myth represents the Greater Personality. Philoctetes, an ordinary person like the rest of us, couldn't handle these weapons and injured himself on one of the poisoned arrows he'd inherited. It became an incurable wound. The stench was so horrible that nobody could stand to be around him, so he was abandoned on an island. And yet the time came when an oracle said that the Trojan War could not be won by the Greeks unless they had the help of Philoctetes. They had to go and apologize for ostracizing him and lure him back into the collectivity. It's a beautiful example of a certain aspect of the phenomenon. One is alienated and becomes an objectionable stink to the collective, and yet he is needed by the collective.

Arjuna and Krishna

This is truly a magnificent example of an encounter with the Greater Personality. It is recorded in the *Bhagavad Gita*. Like the Book of

---

[34] *Memories, Dreams, Reflections,* p. 344.

Job, its central feature is a dialogue between a grief-stricken man and a personification of deity. I have no scholarly knowledge concerning the *Gita*. It is obviously a composite document that grew into its present form by a series of accretions. But I think, considering it psychologically, that it is not at all impossible that it might have originated, just as I think the Book of Job did, in one individual's actual experience of the Greater Personality. However that may be, in its present form it is certainly one of the world's finest examples of this experience.

The story begins with the despair of Prince Arjuna before a battle, a battle he does not want to fight because it is against his kinsmen. And as he expresses his anguish, the god Krishna replies to him through the figure of his chariot driver. First Arjuna speaks:

> O Krishna, seeing these my kinsmen, gathered here desirous to fight, my limbs fail me, my mouth is parched;
>
> My body shivers, my hair stands on end, my Gandiva (bow) slips from my hand, my skin is burning.
>
> O Keshava (Krishna, the slayer of Keshi), I am not able to stand upright; my mind is in a whirl and I see adverse omens.
>
> O Krishna, neither do I see any good in slaying my own people in this strife. I desire neither victory, nor kingdom, nor pleasures. . . .
>
> These warriors I do not wish to kill, even though I am killed by them.[35]

Krishna replies:

> Thou hast been mourning for those who should not be mourned for. . . but the truly wise mourn not either for the dead or for the living. . . .
>
> These bodies are perishable; but the dwellers in these bodies are eternal, indestructible and impenetrable. Therefore fight, O descendant of Bharata!
>
> He who considers this (Self) as a slayer or he who thinks that this (Self) is slain, neither of these knows the Truth, for It does not slay, nor is It slain.

---

[35] "The Blessed Lord's Song" [= Srimad-Bhagavad-Gita], translated by Swami Paramanada, in Lin Yutang, ed., *The Wisdom of China and India*, p. 59.

This (Self) is never born, nor does It die, nor after once having been, does It go into non-being. This (Self) is unborn, eternal, changeless, ancient. It is never destroyed even when the body is destroyed. . . .

. . . Therefore, O son of Kunti, arise and be resolved to fight.

Regarding alike pleasure and pain, gain and loss, victory and defeat, fight thou the battle. Thus sin will not stain thee.[36]

Characteristically, the Greater Personality has presented an attitude that is too large for the ego to understand. Arjuna is confused because what he is presented with is an attitude beyond the opposites. And in this case the motif of wounding is represented by his confusion. You see, the wounding is not so prominent in this Eastern story as it is in the Western story of Job, and that, I think, says something about the difference between the Eastern and Western psyches.

In any case, Arjuna replies:

O Janardana, O Keshava (Krishna), if to thy mind (the path of) wisdom is superior to (the path of) action, then why art thou engaging me in this terrible action? By these seemingly conflicting words thou art bewildering my understanding. [That's the wounding, you see.] Therefore tell me with certainty that one of these, by following which I can attain the highest.[37]

And then Krishna proceeds with what can only be called a very patient explanation. I imagine him beginning with a sigh.

O sinless one, in this world twofold is the path already described by me. The path of wisdom is for the meditative, and the path of work is for the active.

Man does not attain to freedom from action by non-performance of action, nor does he attain to perfection merely by giving up action.

. . . . He who, restraining the organs of action, sits holding thoughts of sense objects in his mind, that self-deluded one is called a hypocrite.

But O Arjuna, he who, controlling the senses by the mind, follows without attachment the path of action with his organs of action, he is esteemed.

Do thou therefore perform right and obligatory actions, for action is su-

---

[36] Ibid., pp. 62f.
[37] Ibid., p. 67.

perior to inaction. Without work, even the bare maintenance of thy body would not be possible.

This world is bound by actions, except when they are performed for the sake of *Yajna* [religious sacrifice, worship, etc.]. Therefore, O son of Kunti, do thou perform action without attachment.[38]

This then is followed by a magnificent, lengthy description of the religious way of life. Particularly noteworthy is Krishna's description of his own nature. Now, I remind you that from the psychological standpoint, what we're listening to is the Self describing its nature to the ego. So this is not just a story of a remote event; it's an account of an experience that can befall any one of us.

Here is how Krishna describes himself, in part:

I am the origin and also the dissolution of the universe. [That's the line that flashed into Robert Oppenheimer's mind when he witnessed the first atomic explosion: "the origin and dissolution of the universe."] There is naught else existing higher than I. Like pearls on a thread, all this universe is strung in Me. I am the taste in waters and the radiance in the sun and the moon. I am the sacred soul Om in all the Vedas, sound in the ether, self-consciousness in mankind. I am the sacred fragrance in earth and the brilliance in fire. I am the life in all beings and austerity in ascetics. Know Me as the eternal seed of all beings. I am the intellect of the intelligent, and the prowess of the powerful. O Arjuna, I know the past, present and future of all beings, but no one knows Me.[39]

Remember, what is being expressed here is the nature of the Self, what the individual psyche may encounter. This is the way the Self talks about itself; this is its phenomenology. The Self's only available manifestation in consciousness is as an *individual* incarnation. Each individual Self, to the extent that it becomes manifest, talks like that.

The way Krishna describes himself to Arjuna is similar to the way Yahweh speaks to Job out of the whirlwind. But it is also quite different too. You see, the whole style is different, much calmer, more objective. There is no whirlwind here. One might say it is more civilized,

---

[38] Ibid.
[39] Ibid., pp. 80ff. (modified and abbreviated).

more psychological. Psychologically the West is a barbarian in comparison with the East. But what Krishna does then is to explain patiently to Arjuna, in this calm, objective way, the difference between the ego and the Self, thereby acquainting him with the nature of the Greater Personality. And this revelation happened because, like Job, Arjuna persevered and questioned Krishna.

Paul and Christ

Here again we turn to the scriptures of another world religion. The relevant texts are found chiefly in the Book of Acts, and I'm going to read you a compilation, a summary in my own words, of the essential accounts. This is Paul speaking:

> I once thought it was my duty to use every means to oppose the name of Jesus the Nazarene. This I did in Jerusalem. I myself threw many of the saints into prison, acting on authority from the Chief Priest. And when they were sentenced to death, I cast my vote against them. I often went round the synagogues inflicting penalties, trying in this way to force them to renounce their faith. My fury against them was so extreme I even pursued them into foreign cities.
>
> On one such expedition I was going to Damascus, armed with full powers and a commission from the Chief Priest. At mid-day, as I was on my way, I saw a light, brighter than the sun, come down from heaven. It shone brilliantly round me and my fellow travelers. We all fell to the ground and I heard a voice saying to me in Hebrew: "Saul, Saul, why are you persecuting me? It is hard for you, kicking like this against the goad." Then I said, "Who are you, Lord?" and the Lord replied, "I am Jesus and you are persecuting me. But get up and stand on your feet, for I have appeared to you for this reason: to appoint you as my servant and as witness of this vision in which you have seen me, and others in which I shall appear to you. Get up now and go into the city and you will be told what you have to do."
>
> The men traveling with Saul stood there speechless, for though they heard the voice they could see no one. Saul got up from the ground, but even with his eyes wide open, he could see nothing at all, and they had to lead him into Damascus by the hand. For three days he was without sight and took neither food nor drink.

You see, Paul was initially absolutely shattered by his encounter with the Greater Personality. He was blind for three days, and according to certain traditions and other accounts there is reason to believe that he had to recuperate for three years in Arabia. The Biblical account doesn't say that exactly, but there are traditions that imply it. I think it's *very* likely indeed.

Paul identified the Greater Personality he encountered as Christ. That is the origin of the Christian Church as we know it. An encounter with the Greater Personality may be violently resisted by the conscious ego, as witness the persecution of the Christians that Saul engaged in before his vision. This is a psychological phenomenon that is well documented and we see it frequently in analysis. Certainly in Saul's case, it is understandable in view of the fact that the awareness that was brought to him by the encounter with the Greater Personality imposed extremely rigorous requirements on his life. He was obliged to sacrifice his personal life totally after the encounter. He became a slave of Christ. He begins his letters to the Romans and to the Philippians by calling himself Paul, the servant of Jesus Christ. He begins his letter to Philemon with the words, "Paul a prisoner of Jesus Christ." And that's what he was, literally a prisoner.

Saul's experience has given us some of the clearest statements that we possess as to how it feels to have had a major encounter with the Greater Personality. This state of being captive is summed up very well in the second chapter of Galatians, where Paul says, "I am crucified with Christ: nevertheless I live; yet not I, but Christ liveth in me." (2:20; King James) Jung made a statement in his autobiography that is not too far from that same meaning. After his encounter with the unconscious and with the personification of the Greater Personality, which he called Philemon, he says this:

> It was then that I ceased to belong to myself alone, ceased to have the right to do so. From then on, my life belonged to the generality. . . . It was then that I dedicated myself to the service of the psyche.[40]

---

[40] *Memories, Dreams, Reflections*, p. 192.

Jung's service to the psyche is analogous to Paul's service or slavery to Christ. The two different terms for the same phenomenon are appropriate to the context of their different cultural and collective psychic backgrounds.

Nietzsche and Zarathustra

I'm now going to make a leap of some two thousand years into modern times. Preceding Jung, Nietzsche's *Thus Spake Zarathustra* is the outstanding recorded example of a modern encounter with the Greater Personality. We don't know how many anonymous encounters of this nature there may have been, but if it remains private, never communicated to the collective, the experience dies unseen.

Indeed, the tragedies of Goethe's *Faust* and Nietzsche's *Zarathustra* mark the first glimmerings of a breakthrough of total experience in Western civilization. By "a breakthrough of total experience" I mean an encounter with the Greater Personality. In modern times, only *Faust* and *Zarathustra* bear witness to this encounter with the larger center of the psyche.

Nietzsche's *Zarathustra* is vastly more important psychologically, in my opinion, because the author lived it totally. Goethe did not. Goethe maintained a certain Olympian stance above the experience that was described in *Faust*. Nietzsche lived out his experience completely, to the bitter end. So it is the first real encounter of a modern ego with the Greater Personality, the first that left a record.

Nietzsche perished in that encounter. But how could it have been otherwise, since he was the first to explore this unknown region, and of course he would be ignorant of its dangers. The dangers only become clear when they have already encompassed you. I think we owe an immense debt to Nietzsche. Jung learned a tremendous amount from his experience. I'm convinced that without Nietzsche's prior example, Jung's experience would likely have been fatal.

In his autobiography, Jung writes about discovering Nietzsche in 1898. Here is what he says:

> I was curious, and finally resolved to read him. *Thoughts Out of Season* was the first volume that fell into my hands. I was carried away by enthu-

siasm, and soon afterward read *Thus Spake Zarathustra*. This, like Goethe's *Faust,* was a tremendous experience for me. *Zarathustra* was Nietzsche's *Faust,* his No. 2 [his number 2 personality], and my No. 2 now corresponds to *Zarathustra*. . . . And *Zarathustra*—there could be no doubt about that—was morbid. Was my No. 2 also morbid? This possibility filled me with a terror which for a long time I refused to admit, but the idea cropped up again and again at inopportune moments, throwing me into a cold sweat, so that in the end I was forced to reflect on myself. Nietzsche had discovered his No. 2 only late in life, when he was already past middle age, whereas I had known mine ever since boyhood. Nietzsche had spoken naively and incautiously about this *arrheton* [secret], this thing not to be named, as though it were quite in order. But I had noticed in time that this only leads to trouble. . . . That, I thought, was his morbid misunderstanding: that he fearlessly and unsuspectingly let his No. 2 loose upon a world that knew and understood nothing about such things. He was moved by the childish hope of finding people who would be able to share his ecstasies and could grasp his "transvaluation of all values." He did not understand himself when he fell head first into the unutterable mystery and wanted to sing its praises to the dull, godforsaken masses. That was the reason for the bombastic language, the piling up of metaphors, the hymnlike raptures—all a vain attempt to catch the ear of a world which had sold its soul for a mass of disconnected facts. And he fell—tightrope-walker that he proclaimed himself to be—into depths far beyond himself.[41]

We now have data that demonstrates that Nietzsche encountered the Greater Personality for the first time in early adolescence. Evidently Jung was not familiar with this source. Not very many people are. After Nietzsche had his breakdown in 1889, he was hospitalized and considered insane for the rest of his life, the next eleven years. He was unable to express himself in any kind of coherent way.

However, Nietzsche's internal psychological functioning was much more intact than his outer appearance would have indicated. He wrote a manuscript while in hospital and smuggled it out with a patient who was leaving. He had to get it past the watchful eyes of his sister who

---

[41] *Memories, Dreams, Reflections*, pp. 102f.

would most certainly have destroyed it.

This is a highly dramatic and significant event. It was eventually published and is available in translation, but very few know about it. Nietzsche scholars are involved in a conspiracy of silence against it because what he talks about are the psychological facts of his life. The Nietzsche scholars imagine that those facts belittle Nietzsche the philosopher. What they really do is enlarge Nietzsche the human being. This work has been published under the title *My Sister and I.* A very unfortunate title, but it wasn't chosen by Nietzsche; it was chosen by his publishers to capitalize on the most scandalous aspect of this work, which talks about the incestuous relations between Nietzsche and his sister since childhood. So needless to say, it did have to be smuggled past the sister!

My Sister and I is a marvelous psychological document because Nietzsche has realizations, in his experience of total defeat—which apparent insanity would of course be for a person of such intellectual brilliance—that he was fulfilled as a human being, and this is all communicated in this work. Someday someone is going to do a full psychological case history of Nietzsche and this book, and he will then take his place as the first depth psychologist.

Here is what Nietzsche tells us:

Of all the books in the Bible, First Samuel, especially in the opening passages, made the profoundest impression on me. In a way, it may be responsible for an important spiritual element in my life. It is where the Lord three times wakes the infant prophet in his sleep, and Samuel three times mistakes the heavenly voice for the voice of Eli asleep near him in the temple. Convinced, after the third time, that his prodigy is being called to higher services than those available to him in the house of sacrifices, Eli proceeds to instruct him in the ways of prophesy. I had no Eli (not even a Schopenhauer) when a similar visitation darkened the opening days of my adolescence. I was all of twelve when the Lord broke in on me in all His glory, a glaring fusion of the portraits of Abraham, Moses and the Young Jesus in our family Bible. In His second visitation He came to me not physically, but in a shudder of consciousness in which good and evil both clamored before the gates of my soul for equal mastery. The third time He seized me in front of my house in the grasp of a terrible wind. I recognized the agency of a divine force because it was in that moment that I conceived of the Trinity as God the Father, God the Son, and God the Devil.[42]

We're talking about an adolescent here, you see, and this passage indicates that Nietzsche's prophetic function was born at the age of twelve. The particular revelations, with their emphasis on the conflict of the opposites, indicates that the Self, in its modern phenomenology, the way we are acquainted with it, had been constellated in him, so that the core issue for him became the polarity between Christ and Antichrist. When you read his works carefully you can see that to be the basic underlying issue. Consciously, Nietzsche deliberately identified himself with Antichrist. But unconsciously, he identified with Christ. So that after his breakdown he signed some of his letters, "The Crucified One." But either way, you see, he lived his life out of a profound religious attitude.

Jung says that the tragedy of Zarathustra is that because his God died, Nietzsche himself became a god, and this happened because he was no atheist. He was of too positive a nature to tolerate the urban neurosis of atheism. It seems dangerous for such a man to assert that God is dead. He instantly becomes the victim of inflation.

Nietzsche was very important to Jung, which is evident in the fact that he conducted a lengthy seminar on *Zarathustra* over a period of five years. Here is a brief excerpt from that seminar:

[Nietzsche] was born in 1844, and he began to write *Zarathustra* in 1883, so he was then thirty-nine years old. The way in which he wrote it is most remarkable. He himself made a verse about it. He said: "Da wurde eins zu zwei und Zarathustra ging an mir vorbei," which means, "Then one became two and Zarathustra passed me by," meaning that Zarathustra then became manifest as a second personality in himself. That would show that he had himself a pretty clear notion that he was not identical with Zarathustra. But how could he help assuming such an identity in those days when there was no psychology? Nobody would then have dared to

---

[42] *My Sister and I,* p. 184.

take the idea of a personification seriously, or even of an independent autonomous spiritual agency. Eighteen eighty-three was the time of the blooming of materialistic philosophy. So he had to identify with Zarathustra in spite of the fact that he felt, as this verse proves, a definite difference between himself and the old wise man. Then his idea that Zarathustra had to come back to mend the faults of his former invention, is psychologically most characteristic; it shows that he had an absolutely historical feeling about it. . . . and it filled him with a peculiar sense of destiny . . . .

Of course such a feeling is most uplifting . . . [it] was the Dionysian experience *par excellence.* In the latter part, the Dionysian *ekstasis* comes in. . . . In one of his letters to his sister he gives a most impressive description of the *ekstasis* in which he wrote *Zarathustra.* . . . He says about his way of writing that it simply poured out of him, it was an almost autonomous production; with unfailing certainty the words presented themselves, and the whole description gives us the impression of the quite extraordinary condition in which he must have been, a condition of possession . . . . It was as if he were possessed by a creative genius that took his brain and produced this work out of absolute necessity.[43]

I want to give you an example. This will describe better than I can the *ekstasis* that Nietzsche fell into:

Has anyone at the end of the nineteenth century a clear idea of what poets of strong ages have called *inspiration?* If not, I will describe it.—If one had the slightest residue of superstition left in one's system, one could hardly reject altogether the idea that one is merely incarnation, merely mouthpiece, merely a medium of overpowering forces. The concept of revelation—in the sense that suddenly, with indescribable certainty and subtlety, something becomes *visible,* audible, something that shakes one to the last depths and throws one down—that merely describes the facts. One hears, one does not seek; one accepts, one does not ask who gives; like lightning, a thought flashes up, with necessity, without hesitation regarding its form—I never had any choice.

A rapture whose tremendous tension occasionally discharges itself in a flood of tears—now the pace quickens involuntarily, now it becomes slow; one is altogether beside oneself, with the distinct consciousness of subtle shudders and of one's skin creeping down to one's toes; a depth of happi-

---

[43] *Nietzsche's* Zarathustra: *Notes of the Seminar Given in 1934-1939,* pp. 9ff.

ness in which even what is most painful and gloomy does not seem something opposite but rather conditioned, provoked, a *necessary* color in such a superabundance of light; an instinct for rhythmic relationships that arches over wide spaces of forms—length, the need for a rhythm with wide arches, is almost the measure of the force of inspiration, a kind of compensation for its pressure and tension.

Everything happens involuntarily in the highest degree but as in a gale of a feeling of freedom, of absoluteness, of power, of divinity.—The involuntariness of image and metaphor is strangest of all; one no longer has any notion of what is an image or a metaphor: everything offers itself as the nearest, most obvious, simplest expression. It actually seems, to allude to something Zarathustra says, as if the things themselves approached and offered themselves as metaphors ("Here all things come caressingly to your discourse and flatter you; for they want to ride on your back. On every metaphor you ride to every truth. . . . Here the words and word-shrines of all being open up before you; here all being wishes to become word, all becoming wishes to learn from you how to speak").[44]

This is the experience of the unconscious in its creative rush of meaningful image. Very few writers can match Nietzsche's superb powers of expression.

Most of *Thus Spake Zarathustra* was written in this ecstatic state of mind. It poured out of the unconscious. The Greater Personality is the figure of Zarathustra, the reincarnation of the ancient prophet. This figure announces a new morality and a whole new world view; what he announces is in truth the harbinger of depth psychology.

Zarathustra is an absolutely remarkable psychological document. The way he describes the collective shadow of modern man is breathtaking. It abounds in brilliant psychological truths, but it is also dangerous poison. It can make you sick. I can't read very much of *Zarathustra*—it makes me ill, literally, because its transcendent insights have not been assimilated by the whole man and therefore they haven't been humanized. That makes them evil and destructive, and they can kill.

---

[44] *Ecce Homo,* pp. 300f. [Also quoted, in a different translation, in Jung, *Nietzsche's Zarathustra,* pp. 24f.—Ed.]

But that is the nature of the Greater Personality. That is part of what it is. That is why we talk about wounding. It doesn't exist within the categories of the ego, of human decency. It bursts those categories on both sides, on the good side and on the evil side. But as a phenomenon it is absolutely remarkable.

Many of the ideas we are familiar with from Jungian psychology show up in *Zarathustra*. For instance, I'm going to read you a short passage which is an explicit description of the Self. See if you don't agree that this sounds familiar:

> "I," you say, and are proud of the word. But greater is that in which you do not wish to have faith—your body and its great reason: that does not say "I," but does "I."
>
> What the sense feels, what the spirit knows, never has its end in itself. But sense and spirit would persuade you that they are the end of all things: that is how vain they are. Instruments and toys are sense and spirit: behind them still lies the self. The self also seeks with the eyes of the senses; it also listens with the ears of the spirit. Always the self listens and seeks: it compares, overpowers, conquers, destroys. It controls, and it is in control of the ego too.
>
> Behind your thoughts and feelings, my brother, there stands a mighty ruler, an unknown sage—whose name is self. In your body he dwells; he is your body.
>
> There is more reason in your body than in your best wisdom. And who knows why your body needs precisely your best wisdom?
>
> Your self laughs at your ego and at its bold leaps "What are these leaps and flights of thought to me?" it says to itself. "A detour to my end. I am the leading strings of the ego and the prompter of its concepts."
>
> The self says to the ego, "Feel pain here!" Then the ego suffers and thinks how it might suffer no more—and that is why it is *made* to think.
>
> The self says to the ego, "Feel pleasure here!" Then the ego is pleased and thinks how it might often be pleased again—and that is why it is *made* to think.[45]

Nietzsche, as an intuitive type, associated the Self with the inferior function, namely sensation, which is represented by the body, so the

---

[45] *The Portable Nietzsche,* p. 146 (*Thus Spoke Zarathustra,* part 1, section 4).

Self is the body to him. That is generally true of intuitives, you know. If you look at your friends who are particularly interested in body work, you see that they are almost all intuitives. We sensation types don't have to pay that much attention to the body; we don't have to deify it.

But the remarkable point in this account is the explicit description of the Self as a second center of the personality, a center that is superordinate to the ego. Nietzsche knows that about the Self only because he's had the experience. It wasn't all assimilated at the time he wrote it, but he had the experience. It was assimilated in the mental hospital—the posthumous document demonstrates that.

I want to put in a few words of homage to Nietzsche. I see him as a martyr in the cause of emerging depth psychology. If one reads him carefully, one sees hints that he deliberately chose the way of inflation in order to learn what lies on the other side. He was a man of immense psychological courage—immense psychological rashness, more than courage, but courage too. Although he was pushed over the brink of psychosis by syphilitic brain disease, in some sense he also seemed to choose it. Here's what he says in his autobiography:

> The legend makers saw Empedocles plunging into the belching flames of Aetna, but this fate was reserved not for the great pre-Socratic but for me alone. Having been separated from the love of my life [Lou Salome], the love that made me human, I then made my desperate plunge into the fires of madness, hoping like Zarathustra to snatch faith in myself by going out of my mind and entering a higher region of sanity—the sanity of the raving lunatic, the normal madness of the damned![46]

And in the same work Nietzsche writes these moving words from his room in the madhouse:

> Is my honor lost because women have betrayed me to weakness or I have betrayed my own strength seeking the power of true knowledge which alone can save us from approaching Doom? Am I completely damned because I am crushed beneath the Athenian dead on the Plain of Marathon?

---

[46] *My Sister and I,* p. 114.

Let Demosthenes, the eloquent defender of Athenian honor, deliver his funeral oration over me: "No, you have not failed, Frederick Nietzsche! There are noble defeats as there are noble deaths—and you have died nobly. *No, you have not failed!* I swear it by the dead on the Plain of Marathon."[47]

Now that this final work of Nietzsche's is available to us, we can see his life in its entirety, as a heroic tragedy, a sacrifice which inaugurated the age of depth psychology and first brought the Greater Personality to modern awareness. Nietzsche's experience prepared the way for Jung.

Concluding Remarks

You will have noticed, and surely it's significant, that three of the four cases I've discussed are to be found in the scriptures of major world religions. Another example that was not discussed, the story of Moses and El Kidhr, is found in the holy Book of Islam. This shows that the experience of the Greater Personality is of such numinosity that it may sometimes bring into being a whole new religion. But now for the first time, in what I would call the Jungian era, we are in a position to begin to understand scientifically, and generally, the psychological entities that generate religions.

This influx of new knowledge is pouring into the modern psyche. Of course it pours into individuals first of all, but it is also pouring into the collective psyche. And this influx presents both a great opportunity and a great danger. It is as if, collectively, we are about to encounter the Greater Personality which, as Jung says in the passage quoted earlier, can make our life flow into that greater life but which is also "a moment of deadliest peril."

It seems to me that our best chance to be spared a collective catastrophe resides in the possibility that enough people will have individual conscious encounters with the Greater Personality and thereby will contribute to the process of immunizing the "body social" against a mass atheistic inflation. If each of us can work toward that end by

---

[47] Ibid., pp. 244f.

diligently assimilating our projections and seeking our own unique in-dividual encounter, then we will contribute to that immunizing proc-ess. To the extent that it can take place in the arena of the individual psyche, it will not have to take place in that dreadful arena of the collective psyche.

In the words of Jung, with which I will close:

> If the projected conflict is to be healed, it must return into the psyche of the individual, where it had its unconscious beginnings. He must celebrate a Last Supper with himself, and eat his own flesh and drink his own blood; which means that he must recognize and accept the other in him-self. . . . Is this perhaps the meaning of Christ's teaching, that each must bear his own cross? For if you have to endure yourself, how will you be able to rend others also?[48]

---

[48] *Mysterium Coniunctionis,* CW 14, par. 512.

3
The Therapeutic Life

Personal and Archetypal Factors

The basic question concerning the relation of the personal to the archetypal in psychological development is this: To what extent is personality development determined by innate, a priori patterns within the individual—namely, the *archetypal factor*—and to what extent is it determined by personal experience and influence from environment, cultural forms and significant personal relationships—the *personal factors?*

Jung always emphasized the fact that the psyche is not a *tabula rasa,* a blank slate to be written on; nevertheless, it can be influenced profoundly for good or ill by interpersonal experience. How this influence takes place and how it relates to our understanding of the innate archetypal patterns is the issue we shall explore here.

From the experiences of our daily life and clinical work, we know the profound effect that childhood events and personal relationships with parents can have on the emerging personality of the child. From reports about feral children, we also know that if a young child lacks human relationship, no human personality develops. In such cases, the archetypal phases of development do not occur at all and the child may remain at an animal level. The same thing happens in those occasional, tragic cases in which a child is locked in a room for years, being totally rejected by the parents.

Similarly, when the child suffers the loss of a parent at an early age and the parent is not adequately replaced, a kind of hole is left in the child's psyche. An important archetypal image has not undergone personalization through a human relationship, so that the archetype retains a boundless, primordial power which threatens to inundate the ego if it is approached. However, sometimes nonparental relationships can fulfill the role of the missing parent. We have all encountered people who, in spite of severe negative experience of their parents, were able to forge a positive relationship with some other adult in their childhood. It may have been a housekeeper, relative or teacher who was able to relate genuinely to the child and personalize an archetypal image. In these cases the parental inadequacies, although damaging, were not fatal to the child's development. Even if these positive relationships last only a brief time, their effects can be incorporated permanently into the growing personality.

One of Jung's early students, Erich Neumann, attempted to deal with this issue. He wrote of the personal evocation of the archetype as follows:

> The transpersonal and timeless structure of the archetype, ingrained in the specifically human psyche of the child and ready for development, must first be released and activated by the personal encounter with a human being. . . . The evocation of the archetype is a personal event in the individual's history and therefore subject to possible disturbance.[49]

Neumann then speaks of a "key and lock phenomenon" by which the archetypal image and the relationship with a human being activate the developing personality. This concept is a definite advance over the earlier, simpler idea that the child projects the inner archetype onto the parent. However, Neumann's concept does not explain how the specific personality of the parent influences the child's psyche. A gap remained in our understanding of how the personal and the archetypal interact.

M. Esther Harding, another of Jung's early students, tried to deal with this problem via her idea of the injured archetype, expressed in her book *The Parental Image: Its Injury and Reconstruction*. But how can an archetype be damaged? As I conceive it, there can only be a damaged *relationship* to an archetype.

For a child's developing ego, relationship to an archetype becomes possible only as a result of experiencing it in a personal incarnation.

---

[49] "The Significance of the Genetic Aspect for Analytical Psychology," in *Journal of Analytical Psychology*, vol. 4, no. 1 (1959).

The archetypal image can be successfully experienced and realized only when it is infused with a tangible, personal content through a human relationship. Thus, a relationship with the personal parent not only evokes the archetype but also provides part of its specific content. That part of the archetype which the parent's personality is able to activate, mediate and embody is the part which the child can incorporate most easily into his or her own personality. That part of the archetype to which the parent has no relation will be left largely unrealized in the realm of eternal forms, not yet incarnated in the child's personal life history.

I would disagree with Neumann, at least partially, when he writes:

> The personal evocation of the archetype is necessitated by fate, so that infinitely more happens than what the mother or father does or intends. Their activity releases the ingrained propensities of the transpersonal archetype in the child-psyche, which cannot be derived in any sense from the personal figure.[50]

This view emphasizes the innate, a priori content of the archetype too strongly and neglects the extent to which the personalities of the parents determine the specific content of the archetype as it is experienced by the child. The full content of the archetype is not automatically released by an experience with the parent. Rather, it is partially released, according to which part of the archetype the parent incarnates and expresses.

If we follow Neumann, the parent is responsible for no more than activating the content of preexisting archetypes. This view, however, cannot explain the profound effect that parents have on the lives of their children. We rather assume that the experience of the parent is built into the archetypal image itself and thus becomes a permanent part of the personality. This notion would follow from the idea that an archetype can be meaningfully experienced and assimilated only through a specific personal relationship—through a process of personalization.

---

[50] Ibid.

The whole process of individual psychological development, whereby the ego emerges from its original state of oneness with the objective, archetypal psyche, can be considered a process of personalization. The experience and conscious realization of the archetypal images proceed only by encountering them as incarnated in individuals. Neumann alludes to this when he speaks of the necessary phase of "secondary personalization":

> This principle [of secondary personalization] holds that there is a persistent tendency in man to take primary and transpersonal contents as secondary and personal, and to reduce them to personal factors. Personalization is directly connected with the growth of the ego, of consciousness, and of individuality . . . through which . . . the ego emerges from the torrent of transpersonal and collective events . . . . Secondary personalization brings a steady decrease in the effective power of the transpersonal and a steady increase in the importance of the ego and personality.[51]

Here, Neumann is referring to an attitude which personalizes the transpersonal in order to depotentiate it. I would add that there is also an experiential process prior to any conscious attitude which personalizes the transpersonal contents, and that *this process is the essential feature of ego development and the growth of consciousness.*

The importance of emphasizing the personal aspect of experience is illustrated in analysis with certain borderline patients. I can recall, for instance, a woman who would be thrown into a panic by any mention of the word *archetype* or any reference to transpersonal factors. She was able to express the nature of her fear very clearly. She felt that any comment that took her away from the immediate reality of her personal relation to me or to her everyday life experience would open up a vast sea of formless, threatening possibilities that would disorient her. She was forced to cling to the immediate, the personal, the concrete. All generalities threatened her with mortal danger.

One often meets the same sort of objection when one attempts to interpret the transference as the projection of an archetypal image. To certain patients with feeble egos, just the idea of projection may

---

[51] *The Origins and History of Consciousness,* pp. 336f.

be psychic poison. For them, the idea that a certain reaction may represent a projection of something within undermines the sense of the reality of the outer world and causes them to become lost in the sea of their subjectivity. An extreme example of the failure of the archetypal images to become personalized is found in overt schizophrenia, in which consciousness is inundated by boundless, primordial, archetypal images. In such cases the individual has never had adequate opportunity to experience the archetypes as mediated and personalized through human relationships.

This vital need for the personalization of the archetype accounts for the way in which many patients obstinately cling to their original experience of the parents. For instance, if there has been a largely destructive parental experience, the patient may find it very difficult to accept and endure a positive parental experience. I have the distinct impression that a person will persist in a negative orientation to the father archetype, for example, simply because that is the aspect of the image which has been personalized in his or her own life and therefore has an element of security, even though it is negative. For such a person to encounter the positive aspect of the archetype is threatening because, since this side has never been personalized, it carries a transpersonal magnitude which threatens to dissolve the boundaries of the ego.

The Archetypal Transference and the Personal Encounter

How we understand the connection between personal and archetypal factors in psychological development influences the way we deal with archetypal dreams and the archetypal transference.

An excellent example of this was first published by Jung in 1966 in *Two Essays on Analytical Psychology*. He also spoke of it in his lecture, "The Symbolic Life," given in 1939, where his comments are rather more candid and informal, as follows:

> I remember a very simple case. There was a student of philosophy, a very intelligent woman. That was quite at the beginning of my career. I was a young doctor then, and I did not know anything beyond Freud. It was not a very important case of neurosis, and I was absolutely certain that it could

be cured; but the case had not been cured. That girl had developed a terrific father-transference on to me—projected the image of the father on me. I said, "But, you see, I'm not your father!" "I know," she said, "that you're not my father, but it always seems as if you were." She behaved accordingly and fell in love with me, and I was her father, brother, son, lover, husband—and, of course, also her hero and savior—every thinkable thing! "But," I said, "you see, that is absolute nonsense!" "But I can't live without it," she answered. What could I do with that? No depreciatory explanation would help. She said, "You can say what you like; it is so." She was in the grip of an unconscious image. Then I had the idea: "Now, if anybody knows anything about it, it must be the unconscious, that has produced such a most awkward situation." So I began to watch the dreams seriously. . . . She produced dreams in which I appeared as the father. That we dealt with. Then I appeared as the lover, and I appeared as the husband—that was all in the same vein. Then I began to change my size; I was much bigger than an ordinary human being; sometimes I had even divine attributes. I thought, "Oh, well, that is the old savior idea." And then I took on the most amazing forms. I appeared, for instance, the size of a god, standing in the fields and holding her in my arms as if she were a baby, and the wind was blowing over the corn and the fields were waving like waves of water, and in the same way I rocked her in my arms. And then, when I saw that picture, I thought, "Now I see what the unconscious is really after: the unconscious wants to make a god of me: the girl needs a god. . . . [The] unconscious wants to find a god, and because it cannot find a god it says, "Dr. Jung is a god." And so I said to her what I thought: "I surely am not the god, but your unconscious needs a god. That is a serious and genuine need." . . . That changed the situation completely; that made all the difference in the world. I cured that case, because I fulfilled the need of the unconscious.[52]

This apparently was one of the early, decisive cases that set Jung thinking about the archetypal level of the unconscious as opposed to the personal level. In this case he gave up the personal interpretation, changed to an archetypal interpretation, and cured the patient. Of course, the presentation has been simplified and designed to make a

---

[52] *The Symbolic Life,* CW 18, par. 634.

certain point: namely, to demonstrate the archetypal image and its urge to be consciously realized. For we who are thoroughly grounded in that viewpoint, I think other questions now might be raised.

In the first place, our clinical experience teaches us that a patient with such dreams is rarely cured by interpreting them archetypally and thus avoiding any intense, personal encounters. In my experience, such dreams indicate an intense archetypal dynamism in the transference, to be sure, but one which cannot be successfully resolved by depersonalizing it through religious or archetypal interpretations. The only workable procedure that I have found is to accept such dreams as an accurate description of the importance to the patient of the personal relationship with me. If I am carrying the projected or personalized value of God or the Self, there is no interpretative way to relieve myself of this burden. Psychological development can proceed only through a prolonged interpersonal interchange which gradually personalizes and concretizes the activated archetypal image.

In *Two Essays,* Jung describes this case much more circumspectly.[53] It becomes evident that the patient was not cured promptly by the archetypal interpretation but, rather, a very gradual change came about. Without denying the validity of the archetypal interpretation, one might wonder whether the interpretation was the decisive healing influence. It could very well be that the major healing factor was Jung's personal interest and concern in this patient and her material. She happened to be with him at a time when a major new theory of human personality was being born. Jung shared this important personal experience with her. I would suggest that it was the personal encounter with Jung's open, human personality which personalized the activated archetype and led to its assimilation as a new part of the patient's own personality.

Jung describes his search for the meaning of these dreams in *Two Essays.* He concludes with these thoughts:

> Was it . . . that the unconscious was trying to *create* a god out of the person of the doctor, as it were to free a vision of God from the veils of the

---

[53] CW 7, pars. 206ff.

personal, so that the transference to the person of the doctor was no more than a misunderstanding on the part of the conscious mind, a stupid trick played by "sound common sense"? . . . Could the longing for a god be a *passion* welling up from our darkest, instinctual nature, a passion unswayed by any outside influences, deeper and stronger perhaps than the love for a human person?[54]

This, of course, is the way Jung viewed the archetypal transference. However, such a view tends to depreciate, and even explain away as a misunderstanding, the intensely personal nature of the transference.

There is another, complementary way of seeing it which gives the personal aspect its rightful value. Instead of understanding this woman's dreams only as an attempt of the unconscious "to free a vision of God from the veils of the personal," we might understand it also, or rather, as the attempt of the archetype to emerge from its remote and eternal realm in order to become personally incarnated in the real life of the patient in relation to her analyst.

If we look at it this way, we will not be in a hurry to send it back to where it came from by trying to disengage the archetype from the person of the analyst. Indeed, to do so might be to cause the patient to miss an opportunity for a major step in psychological development. In the majority of cases, an activated archetypal image can be assimilated only if it can first be incarnated in a personal experience. This is the opportunity that the analytic relationship provides. If we neglect or attempt to evade the prolonged process of personal interchange that must follow the activation of an archetype, if we consider the transference a nuisance rather than a valuable opportunity, then we will short-circuit the natural process of development and return the personality to the *status quo ante*.[55]

Healing in Harmony with the Objective Psyche

This discussion leads to a more general question concerning the healing effect of dreams and dream interpretation. To what extent do the

---

[54] Ibid., par. 214.

[55] [For a more thorough discussion of the transference as "a valuable opportunity," see the last essay in this book, "The Transference Phenomenon."—Ed.]

autonomous dream images themselves bring healing and consciousness, and to what extent do the reaction of the analyst and the interpersonal context of the process of dream interpretation contribute?

This is a most difficult question. On the one hand, there is ample evidence of an innate, spontaneous, psychological process that strives for self-realization. The dream series published by Jung in *Psychology and Alchemy* is an excellent example.[56] On the other hand, there are many examples in psychotherapeutic practice where our own, personal responses and involvement seem to be crucial factors.

I think most of us would agree that the same thing is true of unconscious, psychological phenomena as is true of subatomic physical phenomena: namely, that they cannot be observed without having the very process of observation influence them. Thus an objective, nonparticipating observation of the unconscious is impossible.

This is Jung's viewpoint, and he expressed it repeatedly. For instance, he writes in "General Problems of Psychotherapy":

> For, twist and turn the matter as we may, the relation between doctor and patient remains a personal one within the impersonal framework of professional treatment. By no device can the treatment be anything but the product of mutual influence in which the whole being of the doctor as well as that of his patient plays its part. . . . Hence the personalities of doctor and patient are often infinitely more important for the outcome of the treatment than what the doctor says and thinks . . . . For two personalities to meet is like mixing two different chemical substances: if there is any combination at all, both are transformed.[57]

What Jung describes here is a dynamic field of psychological influence shared by doctor and patient to which both contribute and by which both are affected. It is within this mutual field of influence that all our observations about depth psychology must be made. In such a field it is impossible to make any "objective" observations. Observation inevitably involves participation. It becomes impossible for us to know whether a particular dream or a particular course of develop-

---

[56] CW 12.
[57] *The Practice of Psychotherapy,* CW 16, par. 163.

ment is derived innately from the patient, is evoked by the personal interests and responses of the analyst, or comes from some combination of the two.

The conclusion seems inevitable. No matter how diligently we take our lead from the patient's dreams, we cannot know for certain whether we are promoting his or her own innate pattern of development or imprinting a pliable psyche with our own life view. Since personal participation with another human being is absolutely essential for psychological development in childhood and for healing in analysis, this process of imprinting by the analyst appears to be both necessary and unavoidable.

These considerations raise questions about the essential nature of the analytic process, of the interpretation of dreams, and of individuation as it emerges in analysis. Our fundamental theory concerning psychological development is that the individual personality contains its own innate pattern of wholeness and also an urge to realize it. This hypothesis omits the effect of personal experience or influence via interpersonal relationship. The trouble is that we cannot prove this hypothesis. The observation of another's psyche inevitably involves influence by the observer, This complicates the data, so that we cannot tell whether what we are observing originated from the observed object or from ourselves. We cannot be certain whether we are observing another's individuation, or our own individuation, or perhaps Jung's individuation working through us!

One way of dealing with this issue is to view individuation as a collective pattern of wholeness shared by all human beings and perhaps all life forms. Then it would not matter whether archetypal dreams or individuation imagery originated from the patient or the therapist. If a therapist can introduce the patient to the basic, collective, psychological energies through the therapist's participation in them, then he is serving his healing function. It would not matter whether he has taken his direction from the patient's unconscious or from his own life experience, provided that he be in tune with the realities of the objective psyche considered as a shared field of psychological dynamism in which all human beings participate.

To use the acorn-oak analogy: If we are all oak trees, then it is permissible to share our own oak pattern with the patient, who is also a potential oak. What we give of ourselves will also become the patient's, since we both share the same innate pattern. This concept can be illustrated by the following example of the relationship between personal and archetypal factors in analysis.

The patient is a highly intuitive and gifted man in his thirties, whose childhood was emotionally deprived to an extreme degree. This deprivation led to almost complete psychological paralysis in his adult life. He was an illegitimate child raised by near-psychotic foster parents, and his adaptation to adult life has been precarious. Although extremely talented musically, he has had little opportunity for formal training. He had been working with me for over two years at the time of the session I am about to describe. He reported that he had been given an unusual opportunity to study music, which would require a greater financial outlay than he could manage. His psychological problems had made it almost impossible for him to apply himself to any serious study in the past, but now he was beginning to feel he might be able to do it.

After discussing this matter at some length, we realized that this was, indeed, an important opportunity coming at a time in his own psychological work when he could really profit by it. I therefore told him I would be willing to reduce further his already small analytic fee in order to make up the balance of what he needed to begin his studies. He was quite moved by this offer and accepted it gratefully.

On the following visit, he told me more about his conscious reaction. He said that he had been powerfully affected by my generosity, and felt that it was his first experience of having a father. The response of his unconscious can be seen in the following dream:

> I am sitting before an ancient intaglio of a crucifixion. It is metal, but it is partially covered with a wax-like substance which leads me to discover that there are candles above it, one on each side. I realize I am to light these and make the wax run down into the intaglio, and that this has something to do with the ritual-like meal I am to eat.
>
> I light the candles and the wax does run down into the empty form of

the crucifixion. When it is full, I take it down from the wall above me; I am at my meal. I have taken the head of the image, which been formed by filling up the intaglio, and I am eating it. It is a substance like lead—very heavy—and I begin to wonder if I can digest it. I wonder if humans can digest lead. I realize we eat a little every day, and that we eat silver too. I think it is a safe thing to have eaten, but I am wary of eating too much. The dream ends while I am at the meal.

I have chosen to discuss this particular dream for two reasons. First, it is obviously an archetypal dream which seemed to be clearly related to, if not entirely caused by, my personal offer to the patient. Second, if I understand it correctly, the dream imagery refers specifically to the subject matter of this paper, namely the relation between archetypes and personal experience. My offer to reduce the fee was an attempt to be the helpful father. I liked this man and was aware of his unfulfilled potential. His conscious reaction paralleled my conscious intent: for the first time he felt what it was like to have a father. However, the dream that followed offered different images without any significant personal associations. I have not dealt with this dream in detail with the patient, but I have felt a need to understand it for myself.

First of all, the dream presents an ancient intaglio of the crucifixion. An intaglio is a depressed carving, a negative relief, which when pressed on soft material such as wax produces a positive relief image. I understand the intaglio in this dream to refer to an archetypal structure, an innate form, which is empty in itself. It is an imprinting mechanism that creates images of itself out of amorphous matter such as wax. The dream says that the intaglio is ancient. This would refer to its archetypal, historical nature—something ancient and preexistent within the psyche. The particular form of the intaglio was the crucifixion. The patient was reared as a Catholic and took this religion very seriously as a child; Christian imagery was thus readily available to him.

Christ suspended on the cross is essentially a mandala and, hence, can be taken as a representation of the Self. The image of the crucifixion presents the central theme of the whole Christian myth, which is pertinent to our discussion, namely the incarnation of God in human form, or, to put it in psychological terms, the incarnation of an archetype, the Self, in personal, concrete, historical experience. The Christian myth of incarnation corresponds to the process of personalizing the archetype in psychological development. Incarnation of God builds the bridge between the conscious world of the ego and the transpersonal world of the objective psyche. Without the process of incarnation, the gap between man and the divine, ego and Self, cannot be closed. Theologically expressed, there would be no salvation.

Next in the dream comes the lighting of the two candles and the wax running into the intaglio mold. I understand the lighted candles as symbolizing the life process itself. This is suggested by such common phrases as "burning the candle at both ends." The molten wax, produced by the candle flame, can then be understood as a malleable substance produced by the act of living, which, while hot, will take the shape of the mold into which it flows.

In the dream the molten wax is the raw material, the amorphous stuff, which is molded into a predetermined image. It is this molding process which I understand to be a specific symbolic expression of the personal incarnation of the archetypal image. Without a substance upon which to imprint itself in order to create a real, positive content, the archetypal form represented by the intaglio remains only an empty outline. On the other hand, the wax representing the product of personal life experience remains amorphous, without structure or meaning, until it finds its way into the archetypal image—the intaglio—and is molded into significant form.

Why there are two candles, I am not sure. Apparently the process is a double one. I am reminded of the images of Mithras which show him flanked on either side by a torchbearer, one holding his torch up, the other holding his torch down. The crucifixion intaglio with a candle on either side of it is also analogous to the conventional crucifixion scene where Christ is flanked by the two thieves. Although this dream is not definite, I suspect that a trinitarian process is hinted at here. The two candles pour their products into a third thing, the intaglio, which unites the two and molds them into meaningful form. If this is on the right track, the two candles would then represent the opposites, and out of their combined functioning would come the raw material for the meaningful symbolic form.

The dream then presents the ritual eating of the molded wax figure. This image has a precise parallel in the sacred communion meals in which the participant consumes a representation of the deity. It would represent the need on the part of the dreamer to assimilate psychologically the product of the process that has gone before, to make it truly his own. At this point a very interesting feature appears—the dreamer's awareness of the heaviness of the stuff to be eaten and its unquestioned digestibility. The emphasis on heaviness suggests the solid, substantial reality of what is being ingested. It weighs one down and keeps one close to earth.

One aspect of this heaviness, I think, concerns the patient's psychological type. He is extremely intuitive, perhaps the most intuitive person I have ever met. Thus, inevitably, his experience of the Self must come through sensation, his inferior function. Sensation, the reality function, is typically experienced by intuitives as something unbearably heavy and inert, hence the dreamer's concern as to whether he can handle all that heaviness. In the latter part of the dream, the material definitely becomes lead. This is significant because the dreamer had had other dreams in which lead played a prominent part.

Lead was one of the common terms for the *prima materia* in alchemy; it was the original stuff out of which the supreme value—gold, the Philosophers' Stone—was to be created. The most striking feature of lead is its heaviness, its solidity. It is an apt symbol for earthy reality, and thus would represent the concrete realities of our personal life as opposed to the eternal archetypal forms, which have no weight or actuality of their own until they are filled with content. A similar conclusion is indicated by the astrological relation between lead and the planet Saturn. Saturnian characteristics include caution, control, responsibility and a serious practicality. These are precisely the characteristics most lacking in this patient.

This dream was very helpful to me in ordering my thoughts about the relation between personal and archetypal factors in psychological development. It came in response to the particular personal experience of my offer to reduce the patient's fee. The dream says, in effect, that my offer was experienced by the man's unconscious as an opportunity to participate in a communion meal and to incorporate an image of deity. This is the archetypal meaning that underlies the personal encounter.

Could the archetypal experience have occurred without the personal relationship? I doubt it. The archetype must be incarnated, however meagerly. My simple offer of assistance came at just the right time for it to be experienced and incorporated into the patient's personality.

The Personal Incarnation of Archetypes

Clearly and emphatically, again and again, Jung emphasized the necessity of relating to patients from one's whole personality. Probably more than any of us, he was able to participate vitally in the analytic encounter.

In his writings Jung insists upon the importance of the personal participation of the analyst. However, the passages in his writings that recommend this participation are largely in didactic, exhortatory form. He does not relate the importance of personal participation to his theory of the structure of the psyche. This cannot be accounted for in terms of Jung's supposed distrust of theory. He was quite willing to construct a theory of the structure of the psyche, of the nature of dreams, and of the nature of libido. The lack of a theory concerning the psychological effects of interpersonal experience seems to be a true omission which remains to be filled.

Following his original distinction between the personal and collective layers of the unconscious, Jung became increasingly preoccupied with the collective, archetypal aspect. His analytic procedure became more and more a method of spiritual education which presupposed a well-developed conscious personality. The earlier stages of ego development were relatively neglected and were not given theoretical elaboration. However, we deal with patients in all stages of develop-

ment, and so we need a general theory which encompasses all devel-
opmental phases.

All psychological experience is archetypal in the sense that it is
patterned, determined, by the innate, universal forms of human existence. This is particularly apparent in the young child in whom personal and archetypal contents are inextricably intermingled. It is less
evident in adults because the psyche has undergone a personalization
process which is synonomous with ego development. It is just this
personalization process that many of our patients most desperately
need. The personal layer of the psyche is formed over time, and it is
best to think of it developmentally. It begins at birth and continues
throughout the life of the individual.

All our inner and outer experiences, and those of our patients, are
essentially personalizations of the archetypal. The nature of the
therapeutic task, then, especially in the first half of life, is to help the
patient relate to emerging archetypal forms by providing the context
of an interpersonal relationship whereby they can be personalized.
This can be done without mentioning the word "archetype," and I am
sure it frequently happens with psychotherapists of other schools who
do not even know about archetypes.

When referring to growth or transformation experiences, as opposed to those that result from "projective distortion," the concept
of personalization of the archetype may be preferable to the conventional view of projection of archetypal images. The so-called projection of an archetypal image can rather be seen as a striving of the archetype for personal incarnation—the first step in the process of
consciously assimilating the archetype.

This way of conceptualizing it provides an emphasis different from
Jung's view that unconscious contents must almost always be integrated via projection. Jung's way of putting it sounds almost like an
apology. Because of the connotations of the word "projection," he
seems to be saying, "Regretfully, the nature of the psychological
process is such that we must endure certain projections for a time in
order to work on their assimilation." This way of stating the process
seems to reflect an introverted bias. It neglects the value of the per-

sonal encounter, as it neglects the inherent significance of the personalizing process.

Concerning the Jungian theory of personality development, it seems to me that we have paid insufficient attention to the effects of personal relationship. Innate, predetermined, archetypal factors have been emphasized almost to the exclusion of the personal. This imbalance is a result of the historical circumstances of the birth of analytical psychology. The imbalance was corrected in Jung's own practical method of analysis, which he conducted in a very free and personal way. The effects of this approach, however, were never specifically investigated or given a theoretical formulation.

Somehow, both archetypal and personal factors must be brought together in a general theory. This can be done by understanding the necessity of the personal incarnation of archetypes in individual experience. All archetypal realization is and must be personal. The body into which an archetype incarnates is made of personal stuff, since personal reality is the only kind we can experience. Archetypes have no other way of expressing themselves except through images derived from personal experience. Hence wind, fire, water, sun, moon and stars all serve as images for archetypal contents. But even these relatively impersonal images derive from personal experience. We take such images to refer to transpersonal contents, as indeed they do. The procedure of amplification is a refined method of personalization by associating imagery from our historical heritage with a personal dream image in order to anchor it in consciousness. Amplification takes us a step beyond, to our cultural and generally human parentage. But it does relate us to our cultural heritage in a personal way, and, therefore, is a general approach to the personalization of the archetype.

The personalization of archetypes does not always require an interpersonal relationship. Personalization may also emerge in relation to a field of study or a preoccupying interest. A dedicated interest in science, nature, sports or politics, for example, can represent personal incarnation of the archetype. Of course, a preoccupying interest also can be considered a projection of an essentially inner meaning. But by describing it as projection, we give exclusive attention to the inner origins of the content and fail to assign any specific value to the personalizing process itself—which brings the unconscious image into experiential realty.

Our interest and commitment to depth psychology and psychotherapy, for instance, is an example of a personal incarnation of an archetype. This interest gives structure and meaning to our lives and, perhaps, behind it is the image of the Self. However, can we adequately describe our life work, our prime interest and vocation, as a projection of the Self? Such a statement implies that the projection can be withdrawn and that we can transcend the spatio-temporal realities of our personal existence. I would prefer a formulation which gives more specific value to the personal and concrete embodiment of the archetype than does the concept of projection. The idea of personal incarnation of the archetype serves this purpose.

By using the term "personalization of the archetype" instead of "projection," the origin of the emerging archetypes is left unspecified. This is more accurate in terms of our present knowledge. For instance, in a positive father transference, can one say for certain that the patient projects the father image onto the analyst? Could it not be equally possible that the analyst operates out of the positive father image within himself and the patient responds to it? Instead of a unilateral projection, it might be better to think of an archetypal field in which both patient and analyst participate.

From the previous discussion about the inevitable influence that the observer has on the observed person's psyche, it is evident that one cannot know for certain who is responsible for the activation of any archetype, whether it originates with the patient or with the analyst. The more deeply one considers the matter, the more it seems that in effective psychotherapy, patient and therapist are participating in a dynamic field of the objective psyche, which they share jointly. This way of viewing the psychotherapeutic process seems more conducive to successful therapy than the notion of projection, which tends to throw the patient back on himself and neglects the reality of the participating analyst.

Personality of the Therapist and Transpersonal Purpose

In my work with patients, I regularly encounter objections whenever I attempt to interpret positive transference as due to projection of unconscious inner contents. They will not accept the disregard of my personal realty and what it means to them. Gradually, I have come to feel that it is a mistake to understand the positive transference only in terms of projection. I no longer am sure that the progress of the transference is determined solely by tendencies within the patient. What I am personally seems to have an important influence on the direction in which the analysis proceeds. In other words, I give personal embodiment to emerging archetypal forms, which are then incorporated into the personality of the patient for good or ill.

To put it bluntly, a deep psychological analysis involves an inevitable process in which the patient assimilates parts of the therapist's personality. The archetypal forms are innate in all of us, but the specific personal content which is poured into them will contain, unavoidably, some aspects of the personality of the analyst. If certain aspects of the analyst's personality are too alien or destructive to the patient's needs, these aspects will be resisted or rejected outright. But, here again, we cannot be too certain. A psyche that is desperately in need of some personal embodiment to bring urgent archetypal forms into actuality is prone to take whatever is available.

I am reminded of a reaction someone had to Jung's description of the archetype of the wise old man. The response was, "That's just a picture of Jung himself. Of course he would get such dreams from his patients." Such a remark is apt to be considered a personalistic mistake, but it has its truth, too. Jung was able to incarnate wisdom personally in his relation to patients. Can one say for certain that Jung's wisdom evoked the potentiality of wisdom which was innate in the patient? Or could it be that Jung's personal wisdom was assimilated by the patient, although, to be sure, an archetypal form within the patient was ready to receive it?

We know that psychological development does not occur in the absence of personal relationships. Yet, at the same time, all personal experience follows certain typical and universally human patterns we call archetypes. Although the archetypal forms are innate, the specific contents are determined by personal, historical factors. The process of psychotherapy involves not only the activation of archetypal forms but, more importantly, the filling of these forms with personal content. Part of this content comes from cultural and mythological imagery supplied by the process of amplification. But the major ingredient, to my mind, remains the personality of the therapist. This includes, overtly or covertly, everything about the therapist: ideas and opinions, feelings, prejudices, personal tastes and, perhaps most important, the total world view and attitude toward life.

It is uncomfortable to think that, unavoidably, analysts are reproducing themselves in the personalities of their patients. The only safeguard against the misuse of this tremendous power is that we ourselves be firmly dedicated to the transpersonal purposes of life.

4
The Vocation of Depth Psychotherapy

Introduction

I think we are very privileged indeed to have discovered the vocation of depth psychotherapy. Speaking personally, I am profoundly grateful that I discovered a profession that truly suits me, and I hope that applies to you all, because you really shouldn't be here if it doesn't.[58]

What I want to do is explore the vocation of depth psychotherapy in a general way, looking at who we are as therapists, what we do, and the historical traditions that connect us with the past.

I consider the vocation of depth psychotherapy to be a phenomenon unique to the twentieth century. It arises out of the modern discovery of the reality of the psyche. That discovery, as a piece of empirical knowledge, is a product of the twentieth century. It was never known before. In a sense, it corresponds to nuclear physics, which is another unique vocation that belongs to the twentieth century, and it arose out of the discovery of subatomic reality, which has certain parallels with the discovery of the autonomous psyche.

Both the discovery of the unconscious by Freud, and the discovery of radioactivity by Madame Curie, occurred right at the end of the nineteenth century, on the cusp of the new century. Two unique vocations have resulted from their discoveries.

Depth psychotherapy is both a science and an art, both a theory and a practice. As a science it is a study of empirical knowledge that is structured with intellectual concepts that apply to the psyche in general. But as an art it is a practical one-on-one engagement with a single individual to affect that person's life and development. That aspect goes quite beyond the scientific aspect. It is, in truth, an art.

As scientists, we can say that our goal is objective knowledge of the

---

[58] [Edinger is speaking to analysts and analysts in training.—Ed.]

81

nature of the psyche. It is abstract, objective and has general application. But as art and practice our goal is understanding, which is empathic and related. The knowledge aspect applies to the psyche of everyone, whereas understanding is particular and applies to only one individual at a time. Understanding is unique.

It happens, not uncommonly, that there is a conflict between these two modes of functioning. Jung speaks about this in the fourth section of "The Undiscovered Self."[59] If one is too scientific, then one is overly objective, abstract and theoretical, so the *individual* is missed. On the other hand, if there is too much understanding, the therapist and the patient tend to merge in their empathic subjectivity, and the objective dimension is lost. What is needed is a balance.

If I'm right that the vocation of depth psychotherapy is really a unique and new occupation for the human race, that raises the question, does it have any antecedents? Is it really a free-floating novelty, or are there cultural and psychological precedents? And of course the answer is that there are. Jung himself cautions us against rootlessness. In *Mysterium Coniunctionis* he says:

> Any renewal not deeply rooted in the best spiritual tradition is ephemeral;
> but the dominant that grows from historical roots acts like a living being
> within the ego-bound man. He does not possess it, it possesses him.[60]

This remark applies to our need to understand the historical roots of our vocation.

Etymological Roots

Let us begin with what is usually the best method for discovering the historical background of a given phenomenon, namely etymology.

In the term *depth psychotherapy,* the word "depth" is used to signify the type of psychotherapy that deals with the reality of the unconscious, the objective psyche. The word "psychotherapy" is a product of two root words: *psyche*—originally meaning soul or life spirit—and the Greek verb *therapeuein*—meaning to tend or render

---

[59] *Civilization in Transition,* CW 10, pars. 525ff.
[60] CW 14, par. 521.

service. The original usage of that word was "to render service to the gods in their temples." So in the temples of antiquity, *therapeuein* referred to the careful attendance to cultic worship and religious ceremonies Then, by extension, that verb came to refer to the care and treatment of patients in a medical setting.

Our understanding of the modern equivalent, "therapy," is deepened by reflecting on the root meaning. It implies that service to the soul—psyche—is not just a secular affair; it is more than an ego-dominated business, for it has a transpersonal dimension.

Archetypal Images Underlying Depth Psychology

When we look into the roots of psychotherapy as we practice it, and as the etymology itself implies, there are three major figures that emerge: physician-healer, philosopher-scientist and priest-hierophant. These figures correspond to three archetypal images that are constellated in the course of most depth psychotherapies. We are not interested in history just for history's sake. We're interested in historical roots because history is a living reality in the collective unconscious. When one deals with the collective unconscious, those historical roots come alive and become living realities in the present. Jungian analysts are interested in history not as an antiquarian hobby, but for very practical purposes.

The first image, physician-healer, represents healing knowledge applied to the wounds and ills of humanity, with the goal of curing by means of a particular treatment.

The second image is that of the philosopher-scientist—and I use that double term because the original natural philosophers were the first scientists, and modern science grew out of the philosophical faculty. Indeed, psychology as a science, right up through part of the nineteenth century, was still part of the faculty of philosophy in most universities. So those terms really belong together when considered historically. The philosopher-scientist represents the figure who has the scrutinizing capacity of rational, differentiated consciousness. The method used is the Socratic dialogue. The purpose is to teach and to arrive at truth. The philosopher-scientist teaches by the light of reason, so that we can become aware of what we actually know and what we don't know.

Similarly, the third figure, priest-hierophant, has two somewhat different functions, both of them serving the religious purposes of a ritual. The hierophant operates chiefly in the context of the mysteries, such as the Eleusinian mysteries, whereas the priest works in the context of more orthodox religious ceremonies. The priest-hierophant image carries and mediates transpersonal facts— knowledge of the gods and also knowledge of how to relate to them. The task of the priest-hierophant is to convey religious reality, to provide individual believers or initiates with the revelation or the theophany[61]—the experience of the transpersonal dimension—which has the transformative effect.

These images are often constellated in the course of depth psychotherapy. It is important to be familiar with them so you will recognize them when they show up. They don't come with a label around their necks. Rather they reveal themselves by a mode of behavior or by certain attitudes. If you are familiar with the attitudes that accompany these figures, then you will recognize them. Obviously, it is very important that the analyst not identify with any of these figures when they are constellated, or when carrying their projections.

In our work as depth psychotherapists, we are not physicians, philosophers or scientists and we are not priests or hierophants. We are none of those, although, I'm sorry to say, occasionally I hear somebody announcing that he or she is one. I don't recommend it. We are a new entity, *sui generis,* a new vocation, that has as part of its mode of functioning the constellation of these archetypal images. But they do not belong to us; they belong to the objective psyche. They have been generated by the patient and therefore should be handed back to the patient, not presumed to be our possession.

I expect that each of us has been trained in one of these traditional disciplines. Some of us went to medical school and inherited the medical tradition. Some of us went through the academic disciplines of

---

[61] [A manifestation or appearance of God or a god to a person.—Ed.]

psychology, social work or counseling; these are all outgrowths of the philosophical tradition. And some of us went through theological seminary and acquired the priestly tradition. But since psychotherapy at its roots embraces and transcends all three of these traditions, it means that, so far as our background training is concerned, we are all biased and one-sided in regard to one or the other of these traditions.

We all have to be balanced. Those with a medical training need the addition of a philosophical and a religious education, because depth psychotherapy is more than healing an illness. Those of us with academic training will be weak in the areas of practical patient treatment and in religious realities, because the psyche is more than an object of knowledge, it is also a subject. And those with theological training will need additional education in the empirical and rational disciplines of medicine and science to teach them that the psyche is indeed an empirical phenomenon and not to be confused with the symbolic images of a particular religious mythology.

I'll now speak of each of these traditions in a little more depth. Each is different in terms of the concrete subject matter it addresses, but what I want to focus on is the *attitude* that accompanies a given tradition. That is where the bias lies.

Medical Legacy

So far as the tradition of medicine is concerned, the attitude one learns primarily concerns the care of suffering patients. Everything one learns is focused on that purpose. The Hippocratic oath is really the epitome of the medical attitude in which the physician promises to do no harm, to give his or her very best to the suffering individual, and to regard the treatment as sacred and confidential. That is a very precious attitude that one learns in the overall medical training by living it out every day. It is not just a matter of abstract knowledge; it is a lived knowledge. Neither philosophy nor the priesthood have that same attitude of ethical concern for the individual. The ethics of our field, depth psychotherapy, in this respect are really grounded in the medical root of our tradition.

In his writings Jung makes comparisons between medical operations and psychotherapy. For instance,

> In psychotherapy the situation is no different from what it is in somatic medicine, where surgery is performed on the *individual*.[62]

Again,

> Just as one rightly expects the surgeon's hands to be free from infection, so we ought to insist with especial emphasis, that the psychotherapist be prepared at all times to exercise adequate self-criticism.[63]

And in another place,

> Surgery and obstetrics have long been aware that it is not enough simply to wash the patient—the doctor himself must have clean hands. A neurotic psychotherapist will invariably treat his own neurosis in the patient.[64]

Those are some of the thoughts that come up as we consider the medical root of our vocation.

Philosophical Legacy

Now let us turn to the tradition of philosophy. In Western civilization this tradition came into full manifestation through Socrates, as recorded by Plato. I think we could probably say that the essence of ancient philosophy is summed up by two sayings: Socrates' statement, "The unexamined life is not worth living," and the statement supposedly carved over the Delphic oracle, "Know thyself."

These statements quite obviously have direct application to psychotherapy. Philosophy in its original form was thought of as the instrument for that kind of examination. In earlier epochs, one could know oneself through the process of philosophical examination, which was practiced with a religious attitude. If you have any doubts about that, just read Plato's *Apology* which describes Socrates' defense at his trial.

We owe a great deal to what is called the Socratic method. Here is a

---

[62] *Mysterium Coniunctionis,* CW 14, par. 125n.

[63] "Fundamental Questions of Psychotherapy," *The Practice of Psychotherapy,* CW 16, par. 237.

[64] "Principles of Practical Psychotherapy," Ibid., par. 23.

description of it in a dictionary of philosophy:

> [The Socratic method] is a way of teaching in which the master professes
> to impart no information, (for, in the case of Socrates, he claimed to have
> none), but draws forth more and more definite answers by means of pointed
> questions. The method is best illustrated in Socrates' questioning of an un-
> learned slave boy in the *Meno* of Plato. The slave is led, step by step, to a
> demonstration of a special case of the Pythagorean theorem. Socrates'
> original use of the method is predicated on the belief that children are born
> with knowledge already in their souls but that they cannot recall this
> knowledge without some help (theory of *anamnesis*). It is also associated
> with Socratic Irony, i.e., the profession of ignorance on the part of a ques-
> tioner, who may in fact be quite wise.[65]

I think you can see immediately that there's a clear parallel between Socratic dialogue and the Jungian approach to analysis. They
are not identical, not by any means, but there are certain similarities.

It is also true that the method of science itself, empirical science,
as it has evolved from philosophy, is a dialogue. We don't always
think of it that way, but in fact that is what it is. The scientist phrases
carefully arranged questions and puts them to nature in an experi-
ment—and receives an answer. So, scientific knowledge proceeds
through a process of dialogues. Interestingly enough, psychotherapy
reverses that process. Instead of putting questions to nature, as the
scientist does, nature puts questions to us. A patient comes to us with
a problem—a set of symptoms, dreams, fantasies—and these are nature's questions. It is our task, then, to answer them together, through
dialogue.

Religious Legacy

Let me read you a few sentences from Hastings' *Encyclopaedia of
Religion and Ethics* about the priesthood:

> Priesthood, broadly speaking, owes its origin to the universal need felt by
> mankind of superhuman assistance in the struggle of life. Among all peo-
> ples the belief exists that, under certain circumstances, advantages of some

---

[65] D. Runes, ed., *Dictionary of Philosophy,* p. 295.

kind or other are obtainable from the supernatural world. . .

In many cases savages think themselves unable to communicate directly with the gods. Acknowledging their inferiority in this respect, they regard the priests as the only mediators between them and the supreme powers. The priests are their only protectors; without them the ignorant population would be abandoned to the misfortunes arising from the anger of the gods.[66]

Not many of our patients would verbalize their problems quite this way, but "misfortunes arising from the anger of the gods" is certainly the underlying unconscious dynamism that brings the modern patient to a psychotherapist. In many cases this description is quite apt, even though the patient does not as a rule put it in those words. Acknowledging an inability to "communicate directly with the gods," the patient seeks a mediator in an attempt to gain protection from the misfortune arising from their anger. That is one way to describe why people come into analysis. They may not think that way in the beginning, but they might come closer to that line of thought farther down the line, after they have been working for a while.

In most societies, priests are usually viewed as being *called,* not elected. Theirs is a divine calling. It is not a democratic election, nor is it self-appointed. This corresponds to the notion that the true psychotherapist has an innate calling. He doesn't do it just as a convenient way to make a living.

The priesthood of ancient Israel is probably our most developed and familiar example. The chief function of this priesthood (and of many others as well), was sacrifice toward the goal of eliciting divine favor. The priest would officiate at the sacrificial offering, thus reconciling all present to God by making atonement for their sins, and the theophany would be manifested by the fact that favor and forgiveness were granted. In the Roman Catholic priesthood, this function has evolved into the Mass and the confessional, which is an appendage to the Mass.

In the psychotherapeutic process the confessional is quite com-

---

[66] *Encyclopaedia of Religion and Ethics,* vol. 10, pp. 278f.

monly constellated. Jung discusses this in his essay "Problems of Modern Psychotherapy," Here is some of what he says:

> The first beginnings of all analytic treatment of the soul are to be found in its prototype, the confessional. . . .
>
> . . . Anything concealed is a secret. The possession of secrets acts like a psychic poison that alienates their possessor from the community. In small doses, this poison may be an invaluable medicament, even an essential pre-condition of individual differentiation, so much so that even on the primitive level man feels an irresistible need actually to invent secrets: their possession safeguards him from dissolving in the featureless flow of unconscious community life and thus from deadly peril to his soul. It is a well known fact that the widespread and very ancient rites of initiation with their mystery cults subserved this instinct for differentiation. . . .
>
> A secret shared with several persons is as beneficial as a merely private secret is destructive. The latter works like a burden of guilt, cutting off the unfortunate possessor from communion with his fellows. But, if we are conscious of what we are concealing, the harm done is decidedly less than if we do not know what we are repressing—or even that we have repressions at all.[67]

> Privacy prolongs my isolation . . . . But through confession I throw myself into the arms of humanity again, freed at last from the burden of moral exile.[68]

My major point here is that what one is afraid to have known about oneself—whatever is surrounded by feelings of sin or guilt or painful inferiority—all these inner states constellate on the primitive level of the psyche as the fear of the wrath of the gods. That would be the archetypal way of understanding such phenomena as anxiety and apprehension about confessing some sin or defect.

You see, when the patient confesses such matters to the psychotherapist and survives the experience without damage, the archetypal figure of the mediating priest is constellated almost automatically. A great wave of gratitude washes over the patient. But that gratitude

---

[67] *The Practice of Psychotherapy,* CW 16, pars. 123ff.

[68] Ibid., par. 134.

really belongs to the deity who turns out not to be as wrathful as the patient had feared. Nevertheless, the archetype of the priest is almost infallibly projected onto the psychotherapist who, in all likelihood, doesn't do much more than nod and smile and say, "I've heard of worse things." But that is enough to evoke the projection if a really authentic matter has been constellated.

I think we should all be conscious of these projections. We certainly can't prevent them, but we shouldn't identify with them. In other words, we should not feel entitled to all the gratitude. No, not at all. You are just doing your job. You are entitled to your fee, and nothing else. You see, the feelings of gratitude on the part of the patient will be the sacrifice which, in the older ritual, was offered by the priest. The psychotherapist contributes to that offering by not taking the sacrifice personally.

The hierophant, which means "revealer of the sacred," is a variation of the priest. The term was used to designate those who conducted the mystery initiations in antiquity. Sacrifice and atonement were not the main goal; rather the ritual provided the opportunity to experience a direct and immediate revelation. To this day we do not know exactly what comprised the revelation of the Eleusinian mysteries, because it was deemed to be a capital crime to reveal it.

Archetypal Images Corresponding to Therapeutic Phases

These three traditions emerge during the therapeutic process as different attitudinal modalities. The physician, philosopher and priest are constellated in varying degrees during different phases of psychotherapy. In describing these different phases, I'm going to make the distinction between them quite sharp for the purpose of clarity. Actually, the distinctions are not at all clear cut; in practice they merge into one another.

In the phase of the physician-healer, the key word is *treatment*. The patient feels sick, is in need of help, and presents himself to a therapist for examination, diagnosis and treatment, assuming a more or less passive stance or attitude. The idea is that the physician has healing knowledge and will apply it appropriately in exchange for a fee. This attitude on the part of the patient eventually leads to sterility because the patient experiences the analysis only passively.

In the phase of the philosopher, the key word is *dialogue.* The patient discovers the treatment attitude is inadequate and too passive, and learns that the therapist, like Socrates, really has no knowledge to impart, but only a dialectic method of interchange in which the two mutually seek the truth for the patient.

In the phase of the priest, the key word is *revelation,* revelation of the *numinosum.*[69] During this phase the other two phases are transcended, at least to some degree. The dialogue on the personal level has led to the activation of the collective unconscious, whereby a direct experience of the transpersonal dimension becomes possible. Now the patient and psychotherapist are joint participants in a dialogue with the objective psyche.

How might these phases manifest themselves in practice?

In the physician phase, the patient expects to be treated in return for a fee. Service is to be performed. This aspect of psychotherapy is never completely transcended—indeed, professional ethics are largely grounded in it—but if therapy is going to be more than supportive, directive and guiding, it has to transcend this phase. It often happens that the emergence out of this phase is heralded by the patient's disappointment. She isn't getting well. He is not being cured. Things are not happening as expected. This then gives the psychotherapist the opportunity to point out: "Well, this is not really the way we do business. This is not the way it works. It works through *dialogue.* "

That often generates a certain amount of resistance from the infantile psyche. After that resistance is patiently analyzed, the next phase becomes accessible.

In the philosopher phase, the therapist freely expresses (and the patient fully accepts) the fact that the therapist has no secret knowledge as to how the patient ought to live his or her life. The analyst

---

[69] [From Rudolf Otto's *The Idea of the Holy,* where the word *numinosum* is used to describe the awesome emotional intensity common to all religious experience, irrespective of culture or sect.—Ed.]

does not know what is good for the patient, what he or she "ought" to do. All the therapist can offer are reactions to the patient's behavior, dreams and expressions of all kinds, for the purpose of establishing the dialogue.

In this phase the question always arises of exactly how far the psychotherapist should go in offering candid reactions. We are supposed to function out of our whole personalities, but the fact is, we also have to use judgment. And that, indeed, is the mark of a really skilled analyst—to know just what level of authentic reaction is appropriate at a given stage of the patient's development. Of course there will be times when one goes beyond that proper level and then one has to retreat one way or another. Judgment is certainly required, which only goes to say that the physician stage has not been totally overcome, you see. We still have the ethical responsibility to treat the individual patient as he or she needs to be treated.

The third phase, that of priest, is characterized by the emergence of the archetypal psyche with the numinous images and experiences that are characteristic of this level. It is in this phase that Jungian analysis reveals its uniqueness, for it is the only school of psychotherapy that is equipped by theory and experience to deal with the collective unconscious. We're practically the only ones who even know it exists.

Now, this is an advantage, but it is also a danger. Because Jungian analysts have some understanding of the archetypes which is, in turn, imparted to analysands, there is a powerful tendency for the archetypal psyche to be inductively constellated by the analyst. This is often quite favorable and promotes the depth work that we try to do, but sometimes it is not in the best interest of the patient. Borderline patients, for example, may be in real danger working with those analysts who have a tendency, not really within their conscious control, to constellate the archetypal psyche. That is something to keep in mind. More than once, when I have had occasion to interview a potential patient, or when an analysis has gone wrong for some reason or another, I have referred that person to someone I know who does not constellate the archetypal psyche and is therefore relatively safe for that patient to work with.

In this phase, the personal dialogue stage is transcended and the dialogue now occurs *within* the patient. The psychotherapist continues to offer reactions, interpretations and amplifications, but they are no longer the main focus. The main focus has become the *theophany*, the private experience of the individual patient, and even though the psychotherapist may witness it, he or she has not experienced it. The unique experience of theophany resolves the residual transference and equalizes the connection between patient and therapist; they become peers in their mutual humanity and in the face of the divine manifestation. Jung refers to this development as follows:

> To the extent that the transference is projection and nothing more, it divides quite as much as it connects. But experience teaches that there is one connection in the transference which does not break off with the severance of the projection. That is because there is an extremely important instinctive factor behind it: the kinship libido.[70]

As I have said, these are not clear-cut phases that can be neatly delineated one from the other. They are generally all mixed up, but I think it is helpful to have this schema in mind, because it helps sort out the avalanche of data with which one is flooded in the analytic relationship.

The Occult Tradition

There is an ambiguous appendage to the priest-hierophant tradition in the form of the occult tradition. When priests and hierophants work within any given orthodoxy, they are relatively protected from the dangers of a direct encounter with the archetypal psyche. But those who profess individual contact with the transpersonal have always been marginalized and usually anathematized as heretics or as dangerous occultists by the orthodox authorities.

Jungian psychotherapists are subject to this same characterization by those who do not know us any better. So don't be surprised if you

---

[70] "The Psychology of the Transference," *The Practice of Psychotherapy*, CW 16, par. 445.

encounter this projection now and then. As an analyst, there is also the danger of falling into a subtle, or not so subtle, possession by the presumption of having some special knowledge or wisdom. The best antidote I know to that possibility is for one to maintain a consistent regard for the opinion of others.

Whenever we have a tendency to override a consistent regard for the opinions of others in relation to ourselves, we are on the road to inflation. You see, the fact is that Jungian depth psychology does indeed lead to a secret knowledge—a knowledge that is known only by the individual who has had the experience of the theophany—but that knowledge need not be alienating. A basic principle of Jungian psychology is that we must not become identified with our knowledge, our subjectivity or our experience. To the extent that we are the carriers of such knowledge, it is a burden as much as a privilege. Certainly it does not warrant the nursing of private fantasies of superiority because, in certain respects, it is a defect as much as an advantage.

Privileges, Responsibilities, Dangers

The calling of depth psychotherapy has unique privileges, responsibilities and dangers. It is indeed a profound privilege to be able to interact on a daily basis with the autonomous psyche in all of its manifest modes of existence. It is a singular opportunity to see deeply into the souls of many people, to have all these windows into various living human realities. What other vocation offers that kind of privileged opportunity? I can't think of any. We are immensely privileged by the vocation we have chosen, or that has chosen us.

The responsibilities, however, are very heavy. Because of the nature of our work, we routinely evoke profound projections—not just personal projections but also archetypal ones. It is crucial that we be vigilant not to exploit the authority and power that such projections lodge in us. This is a very grave responsibility because the work we do is done in private. It is unmonitored. No one knows what goes on between the therapist and the patient except the two of them. The responsibility that must be carried by the more conscious member of that process is really immense.

There are also grave dangers and serious occupational hazards. Probably the most common one is the simple psychological danger of inflation. It is almost inevitable that we, as therapists, are going to identify, to some extent or other, with the projections we carry, at least in the early stages of our career. That is a personal danger, because we all know, or ought to know, that inflations lead to a fall of one kind or another. The higher up you soar, the farther you have to fall, and there can be some disastrous psychological falls as part of the occupational hazards of the work we do.

Another danger in dealing with the depth material of our patients is that of getting in over our heads. Especially as a young analyst, it is not uncommon to encounter certain patients who are grappling with a depth dimension that the analyst has not yet dealt with. In such a case, if one doesn't realize what's going on, there is the real danger of plunging ahead too brashly. Then one can fall in over one's head and be very lucky to climb out again. That is a real danger.

The consolation for such experiences—and nobody gets through very many years of analytic work unscathed—is perhaps the realization that they were meant to happen to us because they are part of our own individuation process, coming at us from the outside.

The Mystery of Depth Psychotherapy

In conclusion, I want to say a few words about the mysterious process of depth psychotherapy. What is it and how does it work? That really is the mystery. *We don't know how it works.* We have various ideas, but to be honest and true to our Socratic background, we really have to say that we do not know for sure. But here are some ideas.

I am talking about the authentic business of depth psychotherapy. There are other therapies that function on many different levels, but I am referring to what we try to do as Jungian depth psychotherapists. As Jung tells us, our work requires the whole person. That does not mean that one has to be a completely individuated man or woman. It only means that, hopefully, one has circumnavigated the whole circle of one's own being and knows who one is: one's strengths, one's weaknesses and one's blind spots. That is what is implied when Jung says that being an analyst requires the whole person. Certainly it is the personality of the therapist that is the unique instrument of the process, and the crucial requirement is consciousness, by which is meant the thorough awareness of one's own psychology.

When considering candidates for admission to the training program or for advancement I have in mind four major factors. First of all is the question of vocation: is there clear evidence of a genuine calling for this kind of work? The second is the level of ego development and the reality adaptation: is there a well-developed ego that has achieved a sound adaptation to the outer world? The third factor is character, which involves moral integrity, an awareness of, and devotion to, basic values. And the fourth is the depth connection, having a living relation to the unconscious and to the objective psyche.

As Jung has often said, a depth psychotherapist can take a patient no farther than he or she has gone. Any complexes that are not fully conscious on the part of the analyst will infallibly contaminate the therapeutic process. The therapist will then be treating her or his own complex, projected onto the patient. That is infallibly true, by virtue of the fact that the organ or instrument of psychotherapy is the personality of the psychotherapist.

When the psychotherapist is highly conscious, what seems to happen is a progressive inductive effect in the patient. The inductive effect helps to generate dreams; in fact, the degree of depth connection cultivated by the therapist is very apt to determine the depth from which the patient's dreams come. The unconscious loves to be received, to be recognized. If a patient's unconscious encounters a therapist who really understands the archetypal psyche and recognizes it when it is present, then the unconscious of the patient responds by putting out material that speaks to that understanding. That is what I mean by an inductive effect.

My own experience has led me to the inescapable conclusion that *consciousness is contagious,* with one very important proviso: the psyche of the patient has to be open enough to receive it. Sometimes it can take many years of analysis to bring about that opening. It is a big job to open the psyche sufficiently to receive what can then emerge. Often that opening never occurs fully, and sometimes only slightly. In that case, I would say it is because the patient is not meant to develop any further, at least at that time. As sound empiricists, we are obliged always to respect the reality that confronts us, and, God forbid, never impose our preconceived assumptions as to how far or where a given case ought to go. That is not for us to determine. Such matters must be left to the mysterious working of destiny.

Questions and Answers

Question: You made comments about the defect that goes with the blessing of this vocation. I just wanted to know a little bit more about what you were thinking there.

Edinger: Well, there are some candidates, some individuals, who have applied to the training program and it is determined, for whatever reason, that they are not suitable. It sometimes happens that the applicant feels crushed by that reaction—and angry, sometimes quite hostile, with powerful reactions. When I have the opportunity to speak to such a person, I say something like this: "Look, I don't know what you think a Jungian analyst is, but I don't think it is what you think it is. You're projecting something onto it that isn't appropriate. You're projecting some kind of high worth, some great accomplishment that you're now being deprived of having. I don't see it that way," Or I say to them, "It's a very peculiar business, depth work. It requires a peculiar kind of temperament. It requires a certain ongoing, regular connection to psychic depths that are quite unnatural, that I'd even call abnormal. Most people who end up becoming Jungian analysts have started out by falling into some kind of hole; they have some kind of defect in their psyche or they'd never fall into such depths. Be glad that you don't have to go that way! Go teach in a university or do this and that. Be satisfied. It's not so bad."

Question: You talked about the art of handing projections back. You've practiced for many years. Is there something you can tell us about what you've learned about that art?

Edinger: Well, of course, one of the things about art is that it's incommunicable. But I can offer a suggestion or two.

One way to give the projection back is to behave in various ways that contradict the projection. And if the projection is just trailing a little divine glory along with it, if you demonstrate human frailty particularly, that has a tendency to dampen the projections. On the other hand, if one really knows what one is doing, one doesn't have to be afraid of the projection. You don't have to kill it off prematurely. That is also part of the art, you see, because you are holding a sacred content of the patient's depths, and you want to be able to hand it back intact, not torn and tattered. But the time does come when more human reactions are appropriate than might have been the case earlier.

Question: As we refrain from identifying with various elements of ourselves, do you have a sense of how it is we *do* identify ourselves? If one doesn't identify with anything, where is one's sense of identity?

Edinger: Identity, by its very nature, is an individual phenomenon. You can't tell people how to have identity. There are various collective procedures that recommend identifying with your family, identifying with your ethnic group, your community. That is not my notion of identity.

My notion of identity is the individual selfhood that grows up like a plant from within, and that really is what the whole process of depth psychotherapy is trying to achieve by pouring attention—living, loving, consistent attention—into the psyche of the individual who is in need of discovering and realizing his or her full identity. Ultimately, the seed of one's identity is the Self, and what that is is beyond definition. Jung has tried mightily to approach it from various angles.[71] But it is an experience and cannot be defined.

---

[71] [See below, "Appendix: Notes on the Self."—Ed.]

5
The Transference Phenomenon

The phenomenon of transference was first described by Freud and we are deeply indebted to him for the creative insight that led to this discovery. He used the term transference to express the emotional involvement often occurring between patient and doctor in a psychotherapeutic relationship. Freud considered the transference to be a reliving of regressive infantile patterns of behavior within the therapeutic situation; the immature, dependent relation to the parents being recapitulated with the therapist, the patient's neurotic needs and expectations of their fulfillment being transferred to the analyst. Hence the word transference.

We Jungians, of course, cannot subscribe to this description. I shall discuss the reasons for this later. However, Freud's interpretation of the nature of transference must be mentioned here because his reductive interpretation was responsible for the neutral, indifferent word he chose to name the phenomenon.

Transference and Projection

As you can see, the word transference has essentially the same meaning as projection, and, in fact, the transference is a particularly intense manifestation of projection. In my opinion, however, the term transference is a poor one. We need a word which will express more specifically the intense dynamic involvement that takes place, a word that will convey the transformative nature of the transference experience. Such a term is not yet available. For the present we shall have to make do with the word we have, a term which has gained widespread usage and acceptance.

Transference is singularly difficult to define comprehensively. In its broadest sense, it includes all experience involving psychological projection. In its narrow sense, it refers to an intense, positive, libidinal attachment of a patient to a therapist in a psychotherapeutic relationship where the patient confronts his or her own most intense strivings. If properly handled, this relationship offers an unparalleled opportunity for psychic transformation.

As soon as we depart from this narrow definition of transference, we open the door to a host of other less significant projection phenomena. We speak of negative transference, countertransference, transference to medical doctors, priests, teachers and so on, and even transference to friends. For example, I know a psychiatrist who recently was interviewed for a staff position in a famous sanitarium noted for its emphasis on what is called dynamic psychotherapy. He was successful and was offered the job. The men who interviewed him liked him. But they didn't put it that way. They told him that they had a positive transference to him. This is obviously carrying things too far. When the term is used so loosely it loses all specific meaning. Therefore I will use transference in the narrow sense defined above, with one exception. I shall not exclude intense libidinal relationships outside the psychotherapeutic situation, providing they demonstrate potentialities for psychic transformation, particularly by the emergence of the characteristic archetypal themes to be discussed later.

Lola Paulsen has expressed a similar view which distinguishes between projection and transference. She writes,

> The transference is more than projection, being something archetypal, unconscious, and metaphorical, and as such represents phenomena and processes. The positive and negative projections only give it their appearance and sign. Because it transcends them, the term transference can legitimately be distinguished from the term projection, and used to designate the successive stages of the individuation process as it occurs in relation to the analyst. . . . Projections are aids to the "work," they reflect it but are not to be identified with it, and so the transference of the individuation process goes on behind, or one could also say within, them.[72]

Transference shows different aspects depending on the standpoint from which one views it. To the extraverted Freudian psychology, the

---

[72] "Transference and Projection," in *Journal of Analytical Psychology,* vol. 1, no. 2 (1956).

transference is based on a needy love of an infantile, incestuous nature. To the introverted Adlerian approach, it is an "arrangement" in striving for power. According to the theories of the highly introverted and sensitive Harry Stack Sullivan, it is a tissue of what he calls "security operations" designed to avoid injury by a presumably dangerous and unpredictable person. Sullivan's position, you can see, is a modification of the Adlerian view. Both are introverted, giving primary consideration to the subject rather than the object. Sullivan, however, emphasizes passive, defensive procedures, raising security to the importance of an ultimate goal. Adler's theories imply a more aggressive approach. The power motive assumes that a good offense is the best defense.

The Archetypal Nature of Transference

Let us not forget that Jung fully accepted the partial validity of the above viewpoints. They are part of the total picture and cannot be declared false. What is missing in these reductive theories, however, is awareness of the archetypal, prospective nature of transference and its transformative potentialities.

Reductive psychotherapists emphasize the external, interpersonal manifestations of the transference with all of its infantile characteristics. If they were to study patients' dreams objectively at the onset of transference, they could scarcely fail to recognize the impressive archetypal themes which emerge. Some Jungians, on the other hand, tend to go to the opposite extreme. Their pleasure in discovering an archetype in their patients' material, and their eagerness to summon all their knowledge of mythology and symbolism to amplify it, may cause them to neglect the nature of the patients' interpersonal relations. Neglecting the concrete situation by overvaluing archetypal material can create or prolong a dangerous state of narcissistic inflation. This tendency, I feel, is a danger to all Jungians. Let us not project our own shadow on the reductive approaches of Freud and Adler.

Having said this, we must nevertheless criticize the Freudian view of transference for not recognizing the positive potentialities of the transference experience. After discovering transference, Freud proceeded to describe it as he describes almost everything, in terms of sickness. He called it the transference *neurosis*. This viewpoint has an element of truth, but, because it is one-sided, it is not an accurate description of reality. Freud's relative depreciation of transference is part and parcel of his similar depreciation of childhood, of the unconscious and of the human being who happens to have a neurosis. It corresponds to his profound antipathy to the irrational which he conjured away by applying to it morbid and pathological terminology. This procedure is a civilized version of primitive name-magic and, needless to say, Jungians should not subscribe to it.

The Positive Transference

Although regressive, immature and neurotic elements are very common in transference, they do not represent its core or central meaning. The basic content of the positive transference is healthy libido— the capacity to experience life intensely and to relate to other people—striving to express itself.

The transference, of course, takes many forms and each case is unique in some respects. Nevertheless, general patterns emerge repeatedly. The therapist frequently appears as a highly valued and often central figure in the life of the patient. The basic phenomenon seems to be the arousal of repressed or latent libido in the patient—of the capacity to confer value and love. These life-promoting forces are usually directed first to the therapist who is the agent responsible for their activation. The picture at this stage is very often a dependent and neurotic one—on the surface.

The patient is often keenly aware of the seemingly inappropriate and abnormal nature of these feelings and will resist them vigorously. However, it is the greatest mistake for the therapist to accept the patient's negative evaluation of the transference. This is the error of the Freudians, and its consequence is to perpetuate the state of psychic dissociation which is the origin of the neurosis. The patient's fear of and resistance to his or her own life-enhancing libido is activated simultaneously with the transference. To alleviate this fear and resistance, the positive and constructive aspects must be emphasized, which is often justified by accompanying dreams.

As you know, in contrast to Freudian analysis, in Jungian psychology we hear very little about resistance or defenses. There are several reasons for this. I will mention only that the terms resistance and defense imply that someone is attacking—perhaps it is the analyst.

In fact, the reductive approach which devalues unconscious contents, especially the transference, as only regressive and infantile is indeed an attack on the foundations of human personality. In such a case, a vigorous defense and resistance is the appropriate response. I have known of patients in psychotherapy (not Jungian) who, after floundering helplessly under a constant barrage of reductive interpretations, made a striking improvement with the onset of resistance and the termination of therapy. Something similar takes place in many adolescents exposed to the reductive attitude of their parents. Open resistance and rebellion is then the healthy response.

The real significance of the transference is revealed by comparing the patient's previous state of consciousness with the new transference-consciousness and by studying the dreams that accompany the onset of transference. Both approaches convey the same answer. The pretransference condition will usually be a sterile, bankrupt or paralyzed state of mind which leaves the individual isolated in some measure from people and significant life experiences. The transference changes this. The patient becomes deeply involved with at least one other human being. The capacity to give value and interest to objects and people has been awakened. Something completely new and gripping has entered consciousness, so the patient is involved in life again. In a word, one has contacted one's libido. Accompanying dreams support this view. Dreams at this point commonly include such themes as: a child is born and survives initial dangers; the water of life is found; a marriage or sexual union takes place, and so on.

Transference in Everyday Life

Transference, even when defined in the narrow sense described above, by no means occurs only in relation to a therapist. There can be profound transference experiences in everyday life between man and woman, between two women and, less frequently, between two men. Such experiences may be termed transference by our definition, providing that the libidinal intensity is adequate, the whole personality is involved, and the typical themes of transformation emerge. If such experiences are lived through responsibly and consciously integrated, they then produce a permanent personality change.

This is no easy task, however, in or out of analysis. It is equivalent to the alchemical opus and requires great perseverance, honesty and devotion. Almost always a painful conflict is involved. The initial glow of happiness in finding a dear friend or lover slowly becomes intermixed with awareness that one is in fact a prisoner to one's love. Power demands emerge. Anger and resentment are expressed. Each partner attempts to coerce or wheedle the other into serving his or her own personal need to fulfill the projected image. Angry action leads to angry reaction and the fight is on.

What is needed to save such a situation is the capacity to make a conscious distinction between the human being and what we have projected onto the other person, whether it be the shadow, animus or anima. And often the power of the Self shines through these other figures. It is to this inner power that one must voluntarily submit and not to the other person. If this distinction between the person and the projection can be made, the personal power conflict is annulled and replaced by voluntary suffering.

In the realm of everyday life, I can think of no better opportunity to deal creatively with a transference experience than in the marriage relationship. Needless to say, such an attempt is much more likely to succeed if at least one of the marriage partners is or has been in analysis. Marriage usually begins on the strength of powerful mutual projections not unlike those that emerge in analysis. The difference, however, lies in the fact that in marriage the projections exist within the framework of a real-life situation rather than in the artificial atmosphere of analysis. This fact, combined with the fact that both partners are mutually involved, makes the projections much more difficult to recognize. However, if one succeeds, the rewards are correspondingly greater.

After the initial excitement of marriage, the usual pattern is for the partners to settle down to a more or less comfortable state of symbiosis. Their mutual autoerotisms remain relatively satisfied and comfortably unconscious. Sometimes this situation also occurs in the analytic transference. The patient comes to the hour to bask comfortably in the warm glow of erotic feeling and is quite content to continue this indulgence indefinitely despite the cost. At this point, a blasting operation may be required to move the patient out of this comfortable cradle.

In the corresponding marriage situation too, blasting eventually begins. Each partner begins to see the weaknesses (often partly projected) in the other. Resentments and recriminations multiply. This is the point at which a knowledge of the nature of transference and projection is vitally necessary. If the partners are sufficiently conscious, responsible and flexible, they will be able to work progressively through their difficulties,, withdraw their projections and expand their personalities. However, this is a prolonged task that may last the duration of their married life.

Sometimes relationships other than marriage also provide a vehicle for a real transference experience. Not uncommonly, a close erotic attachment between two women may have transformative consequences. This is also possible but less likely with two men. Even parent-child relationships can serve this function, especially for the parent. This is a field magnificently covered by Eleanor Bertine in her discussion of human relationships, where she calls object love the extraverted aspect of individuation.[73] The psychological precursor of object love is what might be called needy love, possessive and clinging, a reaching out for love and support from a position of weakness.

Transference and Centroversion

For the introverted aspect of individuation I would borrow Erich Neumann's term, centroversion—the discovery of and devotion to the inner authority of Self which frees one from bondage to external

---

[73] [See *Close Relationships: Family, Friendship, Marriage,* esp. pp. 43ff.—Ed.]

projected authority.[74] I would say that just as needy love is the psychological precursor of object love, so the power motive is the psychological precursor of centroversion.

The power motive rebels against psychological dependence on the external object. It strives for independence and autonomy. Needy love and power-striving are two manifestations of the same level of psychological development. They are two aspects of the same thing, two ways by which the insecure personality attempts to overcome its weakness or, to put it more positively, two ways in which the libido manifests itself at this level of personality development. Needy love and power-striving usually alternate within the same person. What is required in such a condition is a growth of consciousness which will transform needy love and power-striving into their mature forms of object love and centroversion. This transformation brings about simultaneously the capacity to relate objectively to others and to function autonomously from a source of inner authority.

Such transformation can never be complete. Needy love and power-striving are characteristics of the primordial psyche which are always present. To put it another way, they are unalterable, instinctive manifestations of protoplasm which is greedy, lusting and devouring. The most we can do is be conscious and responsible, for the child or primitive is always with us. To be unconscious of that fact is to be either inflated or infantile in our relations with others.

In the transference an individual has an opportunity to become conscious of this primordial aspect of libido. Part of this libido can then be transformed into effective energy for creative life and interpersonal relationships. However, the eternal child remains. It must

---

[74] ["Centroversion is the innate tendency of a whole to create unity within its parts and to synthesize their differences in unified systems. The unity of the whole is maintained by compensatory processes controlled by centroversion with whose help the whole becomes a self-creative, expanding system. At a later stage centroversion manifests itself as a directive center, with the ego as the center of consciousness and the self as the psychic center. . . . [Centroversion] operates unconsciously, as the integrating function of wholeness, in all organisms from the amoeba to man." (Neumann, *The Origins and History of Consciousness*, pp. 286f.).—Ed.]

consciously relate to the inner authority of the Self. One must be a child of God to avoid behaving as a child toward humans.

Transference and Transformation

In transference, consciousness and transformation seem to be synonymous. As a new charge of libido emerges into consciousness, dreams of some transforming process often appear, as if the very act of becoming conscious transforms a psychic content. That is, in fact, the case. What has previously been dead or unborn is brought to life. What was only potential has become psychic reality. This I take to be the essential element of transference: a condition of dynamic involvement which vitalizes the conscious personality and brings with it the capacity to experience life more intensely. In short, it is a birth or resurrection of libido—the most precious of human possessions. The dreams and other unconscious productions which emerge with the onset of transference verify this viewpoint completely. Let me give you a few examples.

The first case is that of a transference experience in everyday life without any therapeutic contact whatsoever. It ended disastrously, but the unconscious productions reveal the magnitude of its potential significance, which the conscious personality did not understand.

I saw this woman in a mental hospital when she was hopelessly psychotic. She was sixty-four years old. According to our information, there was nothing very unusual about her life three years prior to her hospitalization. She was reared in the Catholic faith and continued to practice it. She married at eighteen and had five children. Her personality was described as warm and friendly. Her major interest was her family, but she also enjoyed bridge, reading and piano playing. Her life and interests had been completely normal and conventional. The only suspicious note in this apparently normal story was her husband's comment that she was "conventionally cold" sexually.

This was the picture when about three years prior to hospitalization she began having some dental work. Very quickly she developed an erotic attraction to the dentist. At this time, her family noticed a complete change of personality and she soon became delusionally psychotic. Although the family did everything they could to avoid hospitalization, it was eventually necessary.

The delusional ideas that emerged in this woman, simultaneously with her erotic involvement, are extremely interesting and pertinent to our subject. Keep in mind that delusional ideas have the same origin and meaning as dreams. The only difference is that the delusion is of such intensity, and the conscious ego is so weakened, that the unconscious content cannot be distinguished from external reality.

This woman began to believe that she was to receive a huge inheritance from the dentist. There were other delusions too, paranoid ideas that dangerous people were against her. But the central conviction, and the most interesting one, was that the dentist had discovered a miraculous medicine which would prolong life indefinitely. She expected to be given this marvelous medicine by him. Her whole manner revealed her utter certainty of this good fortune. She was inflated and quite out of contact with reality.

This patient was insane. The conscious ego had been shattered. In such cases, deep unconscious processes are exposed to open view. The unconscious reaction to her erotic involvement is clear and indisputable. The dentist is offering her something of supreme value, namely life, or, in our terminology, libido. Unfortunately, this woman was completely unable to meet the situation. Although rather unsavory by conventional standards, her feelings for the dentist included something of supreme value. If the conscious personality could have understood this message symbolically, she would have been forced to deal with the difficult reality problems it presented. She was unable to do this, however, and became delusionally inflated with the conviction that she was literally to receive a life-giving medicine.

Transference in a Dream Series

I would like to present to you now a series of dreams that appeared simultaneously with the onset and development of a transference.

The patient is a woman in her fifties who had been in analysis about two years. Her problem was the common one of that age. Libido for the activities and interests of youth had left her, but she had not yet been able to accept the requirements of the second half of life. She was caught in the limbo between two stages of life.

Just prior to the onset of the transference, the patient had several dreams concerning long journeys or ocean trips to strange and unknown places. Her attitude in the dreams was one of uncertainty about the advisability of making such trips. Then came this dream:

> *Dream I.* She and her sister were returning to the town in which she had spent her childhood. They knew they were on the right road but abruptly it came to an end in a field. Down the hill and to the left she recognized her home town. As she went downhill, the sky darkened until it seemed to be night, although it was only nine-thirty in the morning. The dreamer was terribly frightened but attempted to reassure herself by saying, "It must be an eclipse; it will pass. I will hold on and not be afraid."

This dream reveals the characteristic theme which emerges in almost all psychic transformation processes—the journey into darkness, a return to childhood and to the primordial unconscious psyche from which the ego emerged. The dreamer experiences the same terrors of darkness as does the primitive confronting an eclipse of the sun. It is the primordial fear of losing conscious orientation in the chaos of the unlimited and the unknown.

The journey into darkness, which simultaneously is the onset of the transference, is symbolized in this dream by a return to childhood. This is a characteristic theme and it is easy to see why Freud misunderstood transference as exclusively infantile. He interpreted literally an image that should be taken symbolically. In fairness to Freud it should be said that one can make this symbolic interpretation only with older, relatively mature people. No one can make a symbolic return to childhood unless he or she has previously left it. Much of the misunderstanding between the Freudian and Jungian viewpoints has arisen because two different age groups have been confused. The young neurotic, who is still clinging to childhood, must be treated reductively to a large extent. The symbolic, constructive approach is most useful when relative maturity has already been acquired.

Following this dream, the theme of the journey stopped. She had not gone very far but it was apparently far enough to fertilize the unconscious and bring something new to birth. The next two dreams are concerned with the birth of a child.

> *Dream 2.* A healthy, sturdy young girl of twelve or thirteen is brought to the hospital in labor. The patient sees her lying crosswise on a square bed. On the bed is outlined the iron cross of Germany. There is worry about possible difficulty in labor but the birth proceeds normally.

The dreamer's confrontation with darkness has had an immediate effect. A child is being born within the symbol of the Self—the cross of Germany on a square bed. Although the birth may not be easy, everything seems auspicious. However, the dream immediately following reveals serious dangers.

> *Dream 3.* The dreamer was giving birth to a child in an unusual way. Some sort of construction was involved. Someone told her she was doing it wrong and that if she continued she would kill the child. She wouldn't give in, however, and continued. The outcome was uncertain.

Things have gone wrong, obviously. The patient has injected ego-willfulness into a natural process and has endangered the new creation. This was made clear by another dream she had the same night in which she was stamping everything she could find with her own personal rubber stamp. Possessiveness and ego-power demands were threatening to take control. This is a very common problem. The conscious ego has an almost irresistible tendency to meddle with the natural unconscious process and to distort it to its own ends. This is revealed in different imagery by yet another dream in the series:

> *Dream 4.* The dreamer's cleaning woman, a warm, down-to-earth peasant type, had sent her a beautiful bouquet of flowers. While arranging them, one flower kept falling to the floor and dislodging the others. Finally, she let it stay on the floor. It suddenly turned into a peculiar hard-shelled creature, half shellfish, half anteater, brick red and quite ugly. The dreamer decided it must be killed and began striking it with a stick. It fought back furiously, and each time it was struck it grew larger. The dreamer realized that if it continued to grow it would become really dangerous She stopped beating it. It gradually grew smaller and crawled away.

This dream is quite revealing. Simultaneously with the birth of the child, powers threatening its survival were also activated. The nature of these forces is symbolized by the ugly, hard-shelled creature. This animal represents the primordial, inhuman, instinctive nature of protoplasm. Psychologically, it manifests itself as greed, possessiveness and power striving. It cannot be killed. To repress it brutally only makes it bigger and more dangerous. It is the worm at the core of life which is unpleasant but must be accepted. The emergence of this primitive creature, of course, interfered with smooth analytic progress. It may not be repressed and yet it may not be permitted to live out its desires autonomously.

After a period of grappling with this troublesome intrusion, the theme of a new birth was reiterated in the following dream:

Dream 5. The patient was lying in bed at home after having given birth to a baby. But there was some uncertainty. Had the baby really come? Her husband entered the room smiling, and pointed to some mistletoe hanging over the bed. This proved that the baby bad actually arrived.

This dream verifies that the child is still alive. It is interesting that the sacred mistletoe should be a proof of this. Among the many miraculous properties attributed to mistletoe were the beliefs that it would fertilize barren cattle and if carried about by a woman would help her to conceive a child. In this dream, a symbol of feminine fertility proves that she is creative.

The child met further dangers and uncertainties, but we shall skip over those at present and go to the two final dreams.

Dream 6. She was given a gift by an eminent doctor, a man who at one time had awakened her out of years of torpor, and with whom she had fallen in love. The gift consisted of a round plastic bag containing everything necessary for life, including Time. Time was represented by an umbilical cord in a circle which surrounded the bag.

This was a very impressive dream to the patient in spite of the fact that it contained no cosmic elements—except, perhaps, for the notion of Time. It is a representation of selfhood, containing in itself all the requirements of life and surrounded by the uroboric circle of the umbilical cord depicting Time as an eternal circle.

The dream was particularly interesting to me because it clearly revealed an important inner transformation in her attitude to the external transference experience. I, of course, had given her no such priceless gift. It comes from the archetypal healer. Nevertheless, it is practically impossible to gain access to this inner healing power except through a deep relationship with another person. That is to say, one can contact and integrate the unconscious only via the route of projection. The goal, of course, is to separate the unique and personal meaning of such an experience from the person with whom it is experienced. The projection of the Self must be withdrawn from the therapist if the patient is not to remain in helpless dependence.

The final dream touches on this problem:

Dream 7. The dreamer saw the plan of her life being woven from bands into a large mat. Each band had a distinct and highly important meaning. When the plan was finished, it was a square mat made up of many small swastikas which she laid on a wheelbarrow just outside the door. Dr. Edinger came up the path to see her and, noticing the wheelbarrow, sat down on it and talked to her as she stood in the doorway. She wanted to cry out that he was sitting on her plan, that she couldn't see it, but she realized that his visit was temporary, that he would soon get up and go and that her fear and rudeness were unnecessary.

Here it is shown that the figure of the therapist is obscuring the patient's life plan or pattern of selfhood. The awareness of that pattern usually emerges in the course of an analytic relationship and, at first, is intimately connected with the personality of the therapist. That is, it is projected. In such a case, the analyst may even seem to be an obstruction to development. What is needed is a separation between the analyst as a real person and the projections. Then at last one has two whole human beings meeting each other as they really are. Object love and centroversion emerge simultaneously as two ways of manifesting the same fact—psychic integration and wholeness.

Let me say that this patient has not fully experienced consciously the implications of these dreams. This has been only a partial process, as is usually the case. Much remains to be done. Individuation is a process toward an ever-receding goal, never an accomplished fact. When we study unconscious processes in a dream series such as this we are seeing potentialities. How much of them are realized depends on what the conscious personality does with them. If no one is at home, they will knock on the door in vain.

My purpose in presenting this dream series is to emphasize the fact that individuation and its archetypal themes usually appear, and should appear, in a definite interpersonal situation, namely, the transference. In fact, any archetypal experience can be psychic poison if it is not incorporated into a meaningful relationship with society and with other individuals. As the first case example revealed, it can result in inflation and psychosis.

Erotic and Religious Transferences

In dealing with transference one repeatedly encounters two kinds of material: the erotic and the religious. The same is true of the productions of insanity. We thus have good reason to believe that the core of the human personality is either erotic or religious, or both.

It is usual to take sides on this question and, depending on which side is chosen, to interpret sexual material religiously or religious material sexually. Certainly theologians reveal this tendency when they interpret obvious erotic contents in the Old Testament as referring to Christ and His bride, the Church. Freudian psychoanalysis does the same thing in reverse when it interprets religious belief as deriving from the family Oedipal situation and, therefore, as being primarily erotic. These attempts to magnify one aspect of life at the expense of the other create distorted, one-sided pictures of reality.

[Religious and erotic terminology are notoriously interchangeable.] The visions of the mystics abound in erotic imagery and, on the other hand, the language of lovers is often religious. I would suggest that the erotic and religious viewpoints correspond to what we have previously called object love and centroversion. They are the extraverted and introverted aspects, respectively, of individuation. The religious attitude and the mature erotic attitude are essentially one. The religious or centroverted attitude relates reverently to the inner source of life, to God. The mature erotic attitude relates with equal respect and significance to fellow humans.

Martin Buber's concept of an I-Thou relationship is applicable here. To use his term, we could say that psychological maturity is revealed by the capacity to relate to a Thou—something completely other than the ego. The extraverted, erotic aspect of an I-Thou relationship would be object love; the introverted, religious aspect would correspond to centroversion. Practically, these two possibilities appear simultaneously.[75]

Just as centroversion, the religious attitude, must be cleansed of the personal power motive, so eros, object love, must be purged of needy love and possessiveness. They then have the status of equal principles, or, more correctly, two equally valid manifestations of the same principle. What had once been a pair of opposites becomes reconciled. Both extraverted and introverted ways of life are honored. This is one of the possible fruits of a creative transference experience.

Transference As a Call to Wholeness

Whether it occurs in analysis or in one's personal life, the transference experience is primarily a call to wholeness. The libido flows out to something which it recognizes as its own intimate possession or potentiality. This is one reason for the all-demanding possessiveness of such a relationship. Unconsciously, the individual recognizes that the analyst or friend carries a projected fragment of one's own psyche and one wants to repossess it. If one is able to assimilate the projection, one has made a decisive step toward wholeness.

Transference as a striving for wholeness is beautifully illustrated by the myth related in Plato's *Symposium,* where the nature of love is discussed. I will quote a portion of this myth. Aristophanes speaks:

> Let me treat of the nature of man and what has happened to it; for the original human nature was not like the present, but different. . . . the primeval man was round, his back and sides forming a circle; and he had four

---

[75] [For more on this theme, see Mario Jacoby, *The Analytic Encounter: Transference and Human Relationship,* esp. chapt. 4.—Ed.]

hands and four feet, one head with two faces, looking opposite ways, set on a round neck and precisely alike; also four ears, two privy members, and the remainder to correspond. He could walk upright as men now do, backwards or forwards as he pleased, and he could also roll over and over at a great pace, turning on his four hands and four feet, eight in all, like tumblers going over and over with their legs in the air. . . .

Terrible was their might and strength, and the thoughts of their hearts were great, and they made an attack upon the gods; of them is told the tale of Otys and Ephialtes who, as Homer says, dared to scale heaven, and would have laid hands upon the gods. Doubt reigned in the celestial councils. Should they kill them and annihilate the race with thunderbolts, as they had done the giants, then there would be an end to the sacrifices and worship which men offered to them; but, on the other hand, the gods could not suffer their insolence to be unrestrained.

At last, after a good deal of reflection, Zeus discovered a way. He said: "Methinks I have a plan which will humble their pride and improve their manners; men shall continue to exist, but I will cut them in two and then they will be diminished in strength and increased in numbers; this will have the advantage of making them more profitable to us. They shall walk upright on two legs, and if they continue insolent and will not be quiet, I will split them again and they shall hop about on a single leg." He spoke and cut men in two, like a sorb-apple which is halved for pickling, or as you might divide an egg with a hair. . . .

After the division the two parts of man, each desiring his other half, came together, and throwing their arms about one another, entwined in mutual embraces, longing to grow into one . . . because they did not like to do anything apart; and when one of the halves died and the other survived, the survivor sought another mate, man or woman as we call them, . . . and clung to that . . . so ancient is the desire of one another which is implanted in us, reuniting our original nature, making one of two, and healing the state of man. Each of us when separated, having one side only, like a flat fish, is but the indenture of a man, and he is always looking for his other half . . . . human nature was originally one and we were a whole, and the desire and pursuit of the whole is called love.

There was a time, I say, when we were one, but now because of the wickedness of mankind God has dispersed us, as the Arcadians were dispersed into villages by the Lacedaemonians. And if we are not obedient to the gods, there is a danger that we shall be split up again and go about in basso-relievo, like the profile figures having only half a nose which are sculptured on monuments, and that we shall be like tallies. Wherefore let us exhort all men to piety, that we may avoid evil, and obtain the good, of which Love is to us the lord and minister; and let no one oppose him— he is the enemy of the gods who oppose him. For if we are friends of the God and at peace with him we shall find our own true loves.[76]

Plato concludes this speech of Aristophanes with the following words which I shall borrow for my own conclusion:

Wherefore, if we would praise him who has given to us the benefit, we must praise the god *Love* who is our greatest benefactor, both leading us in this life back to our own nature, and giving us high hopes for the future, for he promises that if we are pious, he will restore us to our original state, and heal us and make us happy and blessed.[77]

---

[76] *The Dialogues of Plato,* pp. 316ff.
[77] Ibid., p. 318.

Appendix
Notes on the Self
by J. Gary Sparks

Jung discusses the Self, and its relation to the ego, from several points of view. In *Symbols of Transformation*, although he does not develop the concept fully, Jung does illustrate, through an interpretation of hero myths, what he later ascribes to the activity of the Self: the capacity of unconscious products to guide the conscious personality. In *Symbols* he presents the view that, as the hero exposes himself to the danger of battle with or descent into a monster, so an ego can be guided and oriented by a confrontation with or descent into the realm of the unconscious. The main and—in the history of psychology—new point in this initial formulation is that there is guidance for the ego from a source within the personality but outside of the ego's awareness, i.e., from the unconscious. (See Edinger's *Transformation of Libido*—esp. pp. 34, 37, 68.—a study guide to *Symbols of Transformation*.) Subsequently, in three later formulations of the Self, Jung then develops and elaborates on this initial observation.

Jung's first complete, and most thoroughly researched, model for understanding the Self comes out of his work on alchemy. He sees the alchemists' descriptions of an imagined physical change in a material substance which "contains" two warring chemical elements—and which is finally accomplished through the presence of yet a third element—as a metaphor for a psychological transformation process whereby both the unconscious and the conscious personalities are transformed through the agency of a third factor, the Self. In other words, he expands and spells out with greater differentiation how guidance comes to an individual from a factor outside his or her control by showing how the Self orchestrates transformation in both the ego and the unconscious parts of the personality. (See Jung's *Mysterium Coniunctionis* and "Psychology of the Transference" as well as Edinger's study guides to them, respectively: *The Mysterium Lectures*, esp. pp. 22ff., 321ff., and *The Mystery of the Coniunctio*, esp. pp. 48f, 74ff.)

Jung's second model describing the Self and its relation to the ego is to be found in the symbolism of Gnosticism. In Gnostic myth the creator God becomes lost in matter when the world is made and must be put back together

117

found in the symbolism of Gnosticism. In Gnostic myth the creator God becomes lost in matter when the world is made and must be put back together again piece by piece each time a holy believer dies and returns to the Godhead the divine spark of God which had been caught in the soul of the faithful. Jung uses the Gnostic metaphor to represent the ego's responsibility for reassembling, as it were, into a re-created Self the fragments of the Self lost in the world—in his metaphor, through projection. This way of conceiving the Self adds a new accent to the understanding derived from alchemy by stressing the ego's role in creating the conditions that allow the Self to assume its guiding function. The Self must both be "constructed" and then followed. (See Jung's *Aion* and Edinger's study guide *The Aion Lectures*, esp. pp. 141, 146.)

Finally, in "Answer to Job," Jung finds a text that yields a third model for understanding the Self and its relation to the ego. As Job had to stand his ground and reflect back to Yahweh the reality of His bestial behavior, so the ego must at times stand firm *against* the Self in order to initiate a transformation within the Self. Again the ego's role in the functioning of the Self is elucidated, but with still new emphasis. Here the Self's influence on the ego is initially experienced as adversarial and only becomes helpful when the ego vigorously resists the hostile manifestation of the Self in that initial encounter. (See Jung's "Answer to Job" and Edinger's study guides, *Transformation of the God-Image*, esp. p. 29, and *Encounter with the Self.*)

Each model represents various aspects of the ego's experience of the Self. Together, Jung's conceptual formulations circumscribe the phenomenology of the Self's guiding activities in the psyche of modern individuals who choose to become conscious.

Bibliography

Bertine, Eleanor. *Close Relationships: Family, Friendship, Marriage.* Toronto: Inner City Books, 1992.

Britannica CD. Version 97. Encyclopædia Britannica, Inc., 1997.

Edinger, Edward F. *The Aion Lectures: Exploring the Self in C.G. Jung's Aion.* Ed. Deborah A. Wesley. Toronto: Inner City Books, 1996.

_____. *Archetype of the Apocalypse: A Jungian Study of the Book of Revelation.* Ed. George R. Elder. La Salle, IL: Open Court, 1999.

_____. *The Bible and the Psyche: Individuation Symbolism in the Old Testament.* Toronto: Inner City Books, 1986.

_____. *The Christian Archetype: A Jungian Commentary on the Life of Christ.* Toronto: Inner City Books, 1987.

_____. *The Creation of Consciousness: Jung's Myth for Modern Man.* Toronto: Inner City Books, 1984.

_____. *Encounter with the Self: A Jungian Commentary on William Blake's* Illustrations of the Book of Job. Toronto: Inner City Books, 1986.

_____. *The Mysterium Lectures: A Journey Through C.G. Jung's* Mysterium Coniunctionis. Ed. Joan Dexter Blackmer. Toronto: Inner City Books, 1995.

_____. *The Mystery of the Coniunctio: Alchemical Image of Individuation.* Ed. Joan Dexter Blackmer. Toronto: Inner City Books, 1994.

_____. *Transformation of the God-Image: An Elucidation of Jung's* Answer to Job. Ed. Lawrence W. Jaffe. Toronto: Inner City Books, 1992.

_____. *Transformation of Libido: A Seminar on C.G. Jung's* Symbols of Transformation. Ed. Dianne D. Cordic. Los Angeles: C.G. Jung Bookstore, 1994.

Emerson, Ralph Waldo. *Emerson's Essays.* New York: Harper and Row, 1951.

Harding, M. Esther. *The Parental Image: Its Injury and Reconstruction.* New York: Putnams, 1965. [Also Toronto: Inner City Books, 2003 (in preparation).]

Hastings, James, ed. *Encyclopedia of Religion and Ethics.* 12 vols. New York: Charles Scribner's Sons, 1917-1927.

Jacoby, Mario. *The Analytic Encounter: Transference and Human Relationship.* Toronto: Inner City Books, 1984.

Jung, C.G. *The Collected Works* (Bollingen Series XX). 20 vols. Trans. R.F.C. Hull. Ed. H. Read, M. Fordham, G. Adler, Wm. McGuire. Princeton: Princeton University Press, 1953-1979.

_____. *Letters* (Bolligen Series XCV). 2 vols. Trans. R.F.C. Hull. Ed. G. Adler, A. Jaffé. Princeton: Princeton University Press, 1973.

_____. *Memories, Dreams, Reflections*. Ed. Aniela Jaffé. New York: Random House, 1963.

_____. *Nietzsche's* Zarathustra: *Notes of the Seminar Given in 1934-1939* (Bollingen Series XCIX). 2 vols. Ed. James L. Jarrett. Princeton: Princeton University Press, 1988.

_____. *Seminar 1925*. Mimeographed Notes of Seminar, March 23 - July 6, 1925. Zurich.

McGuire, William, and Hull, R.F.C., eds. *C.G. Jung Speaking* (Bollingen Series XCVII). Princeton: Princeton University Press, 1977.

Neumann, Erich. The Origins and History of Consciousness (Bollingen Series XLII). Princeton: Princeton University Press, 1973.

_____. "The Significance of the Genetic Aspect for Analytical Psychology." In *Journal of Analytical Psychology,* vol. 4, no. 1 (1959).

Nietzsche, Friedrich. *Ecce Homo.* Trans. Walter Kaufmann.. New York: Vintage Books, 1969.

_____. *My Sister and I.* Trans. O. Levy. Los Angeles: Amok Books, 1990.

_____. *The Portable Nietzsche.* Trans. Walter Kaufmann. New York: Viking Press, 1954.

Otto, Rudolf. *The Idea of the Holy.* Trans. John W. Harvey. London: Oxford University Press, 1958.

Paulsen, Lola. "Transference and Projection." In *Journal of Analytical Psychology,* vol. 1, no. 2 (1956).

Plato. *The Dialogues of Plato.* Trans. B. Jowett. New York: Random House, 1937.

Runes, Dagobert D., ed. *Dictionary of Philosophy.* Totowa, NJ: Littlefield, Adams & Co., 1971.

Yutang, Lin, ed. *The Wisdom of China and India.* New York: Random House/ Modern Library, 1942.

Index

Page nos. in *italic* refer to illustrations

Also by Edward F. Edinger in this series

THE PSYCHE ON STAGE
Individuation Motifs in Shakespeare and Sophocles
ISBN 0-919123-94-5. (2001) 96 pp. **Illustrated** $16

EGO AND SELF
The Old Testament Prophets
ISBN 0-919123-91-0. (2000) 160 pp. $16

THE PSYCHE IN ANTIQUITY
  Book 1: Early Greek Philosophy
  ISBN 0-919123-86-4. (1999) 128 pp. $16
  Book 2: Gnosticism and Early Christianity
  ISBN 0-919123-87-2. (1999) 160 pp. $16

THE AION LECTURES: Exploring the Self in Jung's *Aion*
ISBN 0-919123-72-4. (1996) 208 pp. **30 illustrations** $18

MELVILLE'S MOBY-DICK: An American Nekyia
ISBN 0-919123-70-8. (1995) 160 pp. $16

THE MYSTERIUM LECTURES
A Journey Through Jung's *Mysterium Coniunctionis*
ISBN 0-919123-66-X. (1995) 352 pp. **90 illustrations** $25

THE MYSTERY OF THE CONIUNCTIO
Alchemical Image of Individuation
ISBN 0-919123-67-8. (1994) 112 pp. **48 illustrations** $16

GOETHE'S FAUST: Notes for a Jungian Commentary
ISBN 0-919123-44-9. (1990) 112 pp. $16

THE CHRISTIAN ARCHETYPE
A Jungian Commentary on the Life of Christ
ISBN 0-919123-27-9. (1987) 144 pp. **34 illustrations** $16

THE BIBLE AND THE PSYCHE
Individuation Symbolism in the Old Testament
ISBN 0-919123-23-6. (1986) 176 pp. $18

ENCOUNTER WITH THE SELF
A Jungian Commentary on William Blake's *Illustrations of the Book of Job*
ISBN 0-919123-21-X. (1986) 80 pp. **22 illustrations** $15

THE CREATION OF CONSCIOUSNESS
Jung's Myth for Modern Man
ISBN 0-919123-13-9. (1984) 128 pp. **10 illustrations** $16

Studies in Jungian Psychology
by Jungian Analysts

Quality Paperbacks

Prices and payment in $US (except in Canada, $Cdn)

The Secret Raven: Conflict and Transformation
Daryl Sharp (Toronto). ISBN 0-919123-00-7. 128 pp. $16

The Psychological Meaning of Redemption Motifs in Fairy Tales
Marie-Louise von Franz (Zürich). ISBN 0-919123-01-5. 128 pp. $16

Alchemy: An Introduction to the Symbolism and the Psychology
Marie-Louise von Franz (Zürich). ISBN 0-919123-04-X. 288 pp. $20

Descent to the Goddess: A Way of Initiation for Women
Sylvia Brinton Perera (New York). ISBN 0-919123-05-8. 112 pp. $16

Addiction to Perfection: The Still Unravished Bride
Marion Woodman (Toronto). ISBN 0-919123-11-2. 208 pp. $18pb/$25hc

Jungian Dream Interpretation: A Handbook of Theory and Practice
James A. Hall, M.D. (Dallas). ISBN 0-919123-12-0. 128 pp. $16

The Creation of Consciousness: Jung's Myth for Modern Man
Edward F. Edinger (Los Angeles). ISBN 0-919123-13-9. 128 pp. $16

The Analytic Encounter: Transference and Human Relationship
Mario Jacoby (Zürich). ISBN 0-919123-14-7. 128 pp. $16

Change of Life: Dreams and the Menopause
Ann Mankowitz (Ireland). ISBN 0-919123-15-5. 128 pp. $16

The Illness That We Are: A Jungian Critique of Christianity
John P. Dourley (Ottawa). ISBN 0-919123-16-3. 128 pp. $16

Cultural Attitudes in Psychological Perspective
Joseph L. Henderson, M.D. (San Francisco). ISBN 0-919123-18-X. 128 pp. $16

The Vertical Labyrinth: Individuation in Jungian Psychology
Aldo Carotenuto (Rome). ISBN 0-919123-19-8. 144 pp. $16

The Pregnant Virgin: A Process of Psychological Transformation
Marion Woodman (Toronto). ISBN 0-919123-20-1. 208 pp. $18pb/$25hc

Encounter with the Self: William Blake's *Illustrations of the Book of Job*
Edward F. Edinger (Los Angeles). ISBN 0-919123-21-X. 80 pp. $15

The Scapegoat Complex: Toward a Mythology of Shadow and Guilt
Sylvia Brinton Perera (New York). ISBN 0-919123-22-8. 128 pp. $16

The Jungian Experience: Analysis and Individuation
James A. Hall, M.D. (Dallas). ISBN 0-919123-25-2. 176 pp. $18

Phallos: Sacred Image of the Masculine
Eugene Monick (Scranton, PA). ISBN 0-919123-26-0. 144 pp. $16

Touching: Body Therapy and Depth Psychology
Deldon Anne McNeely (Lynchburg, VA). ISBN 0-919123-29-5. 128 pp. $16

Personality Types: Jung's Model of Typology
Daryl Sharp (Toronto). ISBN 0-919123-30-9. 128 pp. $16

The Sacred Prostitute: Eternal Aspect of the Feminine
Nancy Qualls-Corbett (Birmingham). ISBN 0-919123-31-7. 176 pp. $18

When the Spirits Come Back
Janet O. Dallett (Seal Harbor, WA). ISBN 0-919123-32-5. 160 pp. $16

The Mother: Archetypal Image in Fairy Tales
Sibylle Birkhäuser-Oeri (Zürich). ISBN 0-919123-33-3. 176 pp. $18

The Survival Papers: Anatomy of a Midlife Crisis
Daryl Sharp (Toronto). ISBN 0-919123-34-1. 160 pp. $16

The Cassandra Complex: Living with Disbelief
Laurie Layton Schapira (New York). ISBN 0-919123-35-X. 160 pp. $16

Acrobats of the Gods: Dance and Transformation
Joan Dexter Blackmer (Wilmot Flat, NH). ISBN 0-919123-38-4. 128 pp. $16

Eros and Pathos: Shades of Love and Suffering
Aldo Carotenuto (Rome). ISBN 0-919123-39-2. 160 pp. $16

The Ravaged Bridegroom: Masculinity in Women
Marion Woodman (Toronto). ISBN 0-919123-42-2. 224 pp. $20

Liberating the Heart: Spirituality and Jungian Psychology
Lawrence W. Jaffe (Berkeley). ISBN 0-919123-43-0. 176 pp. $18

The Dream Story
Donald Broadribb (Baker's Hill, Australia). ISBN 0-919123-45-7. 256 pp. $20

The Rainbow Serpent: Bridge to Consciousness
Robert L. Gardner (Toronto). ISBN 0-919123-46-5. 128 pp. $16

Circle of Care: Clinical Issues in Jungian Therapy
Warren Steinberg (New York). ISBN 0-919123-47-3. 160 pp. $16

Jung Lexicon: A Primer of Terms & Concepts
Daryl Sharp (Toronto). ISBN 0-919123-48-1. 160 pp. $16

Body and Soul: The Other Side of Illness
Albert Kreinheder (Los Angeles). ISBN 0-919123-49-X. 112 pp. $16

The Secret Lore of Gardening: Patterns of Male Intimacy
Graham Jackson (Toronto). ISBN 0-919123-53-8. 160 pp. $16

Getting To Know You: The Inside Out of Relationship
Daryl Sharp (Toronto). ISBN 0-919123-56-2. 128 pp. $16

Conscious Femininity: Interviews with Marion Woodman
Introduction by Marion Woodman (Toronto). ISBN 0-919123-59-7. 160 pp. $16

The Middle Passage: From Misery to Meaning in Midlife
James Hollis (Houston). ISBN 0-919123-60-0. 128 pp. $16

Chicken Little: The Inside Story *(A Jungian Romance)*
Daryl Sharp (Toronto). ISBN 0-919123-62-7. 128 pp. $16

Coming To Age: The Croning Years and Late-Life Transformation
Jane R. Prétat (Providence, RI). ISBN 0-919123-63-5. 144 pp. $16

Under Saturn's Shadow: The Wounding and Healing of Men
James Hollis (Houston). ISBN 0-919123-64-3. 144 pp. $16

Discounts: any 3-5 books, 10%; 6-9 books, 20%; 10 or more, 25%
Add Postage/Handling: 1-2 books, $3; 3-4 books, $5; 5-9 books, $10; 10 or more, free

Write or phone for free Catalogue of **over 100 titles** and **Jung at Heart** newsletter

INNER CITY BOOKS, Box 1271, Station Q, Toronto, ON M4T 2P4, Canada
Tel. 416- 927-0355 / Fax 416-924-1814 / E-mail info@innercitybooks.net